Simple & Stylish Patterns
FOR DOLLS' HATS & SHOES

Creative Crafters

Simple & Stylish Patterns
for
DOLLS' HATS & SHOES

for 18-inch, 14-inch and 8-inch dolls

by Marla Freeman

Portfolio Press

First edition/First printing

To purchase additional copies of this book, please contact:
Portfolio Press, 130 Wineow Street, Cumberland, MD 21502
877-737-1200

Library of Congress Catalog Card Number 00-131630
ISBN 0-942620-42-9

Project Editor: Cary Raesner
Editorial Consultant: Virginia Ann Heyerdahl
Interior Photography: Tenrec Research
Patterns: Allison Rothe
Cover Design: Kourtney Mills
Design and Production: Tammy S. Blank

Ginny Miss 1920's courtesy of The Vogue Doll Company, Inc.
Corolle toddler doll courtesy of Corolle
Magic Attic Heather doll courtesy of Anna Goddu

Cover and page 2 photos by Sepp Seitz

Printed and bound in the United States of America

Contents

See page 74 for instructions.

See page 18 for instructions.

See page 24 for instructions.

See page 30 for instructions.

See page 36 for instructions.

See page 44 for instructions.

See page 50 for instructions.

See page 56 for instructions.

See page 62 for instructions.

See page 68 for instructions.

See page 80 for instructions.

See page 86 for instructions.

Introduction

We've designed an imaginative collection of hats and footwear to complete, or complement, your dolls' favorite outfits. Each of these twelve sets includes instructions and patterns to fit an 18-inch, 14-inch and 8-inch doll.

The Fleece Hat and Oxfords will add the finishing touch to a casual, late-fall outfit. Keep the Rain Hat and Puddle Jumpers handy for showers and storms. Our dapper Beret and Mary Janes are classics that never go out of style.

When you dress your doll for summer fun, consider the Camp Hat and Moccasins or Sunflower Hat and Ankle-Strap Shoes. The Summer Hat and Shoes are perfect for warm days at the beach or picnicking, and present the opportunity to clothe your dolls in bright colorful fabrics from top to bottom. If your doll is going on a cruise, finish her ensemble with a Sailor Hat and Canvas Slip-ons. You might add the Baseball Cap and Sneakers to any casual outfit in the fall or spring as well as summer.

Special days and events call for special accessories. A warm-weather celebration calls for the Dainty Spring Bonnet and Mary Janes; the T-Strap shoes and Communion Veil are perfect for that once-in-a-lifetime experience. Feel free to create your own combinations—the T-Strap shoes are also a good match with the be-flowered Dainty Spring Bonnet. If your doll loves to dance, complete her ballet costume with the Feathered Headpiece and Ballet Slippers or the Top Hat and Tap Shoes.

Many of these hats and shoes can be made from fabric scraps and trims you have stashed in your sewing room or cupboard. These projects are also ideal for using "found" items. You may choose to purchase new fabric, or you may search in thrift shops for fabric or trim in just the right color or texture. Worn coats, jackets, purses, gloves or boots can also be a good source of vinyl or leather to create one of these outfits.

Measurements are important. Not all 18-inch, 14-inch or 8-inch dolls are created equal. We have modeled these ensembles on an 18-inch Magic Attic doll, a 14-inch Corolle toddler and an 8-inch Ginny, but the patterns can be modified to fit dolls (or even plush animals) that are in the same approximate size range.

If your dolls don't have ensembles to go with a hat-and-shoe combination that has caught your fancy, consider creating new outfits for your doll to match *them*! Remember, if the shoe fits....

Baseball Cap & Sneakers

Materials for Baseball Cap

- 1/4 yard [1/8 yard for 8-inch size] twill fabric
- 1/4 yard [1/8 yard for 8-inch size] heavy interfacing
- 1/4 yard [1/8 yard for 8-inch size] fusible web
- 13 inches [10 inches for 14-inch size, 9 inches for 8-inch size] matching bias binding
- Sewing needle
- Matching thread

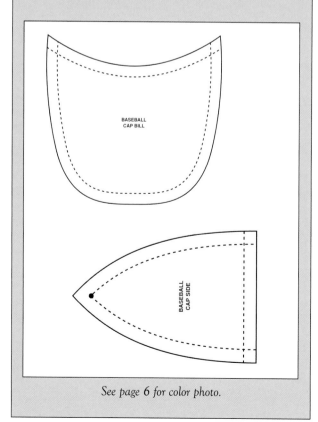

See page 6 for color photo.

Materials for Sneakers

- 1/4 yard [1/8 yard for 8-inch size] twill fabric
- 1/4 yard [1/8 yard for 8-inch size] flannel fabric
- 1/4 yard [1/8 yard for 8-inch size] fusible web
- Matching or contrasting double-fold bias tape
- Scrap of extra-thick craft foam
- Lightweight cardboard
- Small round shoelaces
- Fabric glue
- Sewing needle
- Matching thread
- Spring clothespins
- Sharp pointed tool

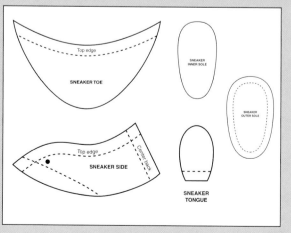

See page 6 for color photo.

Baseball Cap

Sizes: To fit 18-inch, 14-inch and 8-inch dolls

Note: Instructions are given for the 18-inch size, with requirements for smaller sizes shown in brackets when applicable. When only one requirement is given, it applies to all three sizes.

Pattern Notes

Use 1/4-inch [1/8-inch for 8-inch size] seam allowance throughout unless indicated otherwise.

Set machine stitch size to 10–12 stitches per inch.

Clip all seams and curves, as indicated on pattern.

Use zigzag or edging stitch to finish raw edges.

Cutting Instructions

1. Cut one baseball cap bill from twill fabric. Trace six baseball cap sides and one baseball cap bill onto paper side of fusible web; cut out just outside traced lines. Following manufacturer's instructions, apply to wrong side of twill fabric; cut out on traced lines.

2. Remove paper backing; apply bonded twill pieces to heavy interfacing; cut out.

Sewing Instructions

1. Topstitch each side piece 3/8-inch from each side edge.

2. With right sides together, sew two side pieces together from dot at top to bottom edge. Trim seam to 1/8-inch; finish raw edge. Sew a third side piece to first two in same manner.

3. Repeat step 2 with remaining three side pieces.

4. With right sides together, sew joined side pieces together from one bottom edge, across top and down to opposite bottom edge. Trim seam to 1/8-inch; finish raw edge. Turn right side out.

5. With right sides together, sew baseball cap bills together around outer edge. Trim seams; turn right side out. Press.

6. Topstitch bill approximately 1/4-inch [1/8-inch for 8-inch size] from outer edge. Repeat top stitching at equal intervals to center of bill.

7. Make a 1/4-inch [1/8-inch for 8-inch size] seam across inner edge; clip curves to stitching across edge. With raw edges even, baste bill to sides of cap; stitch.

8. Open fold on one edge of bias binding; turn under 1/4-inch [1/8-inch for 8-inch size] on one end. With right sides together, and open edge of binding even with raw edge of cap sides, sew binding around bottom of sides and over inner edge of bill, overlapping ends of binding.

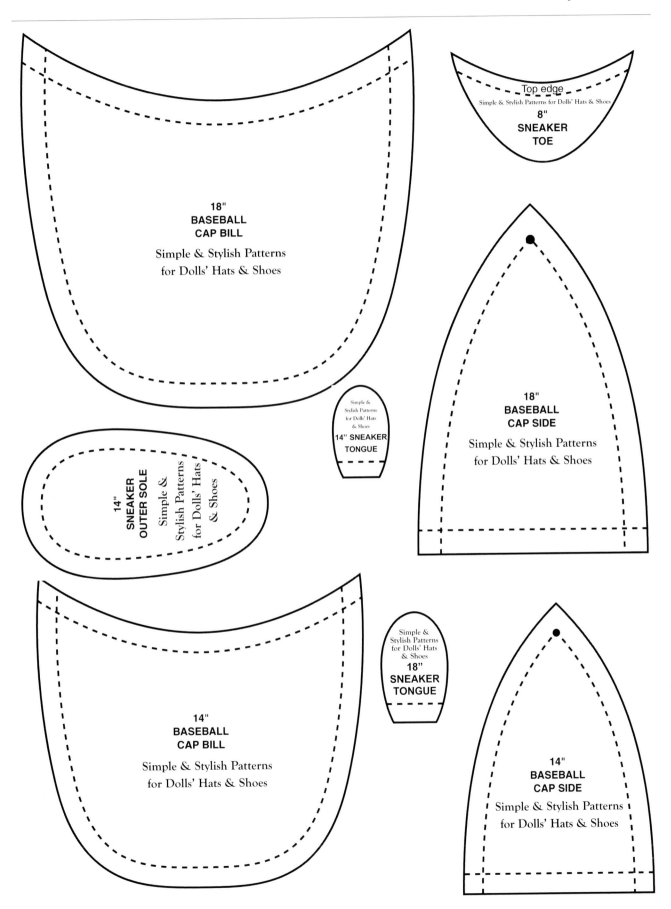

18"
BASEBALL
CAP BILL

Simple & Stylish Patterns
for Dolls' Hats & Shoes

Top edge
Simple & Stylish Patterns for Dolls' Hats & Shoes
8"
SNEAKER
TOE

Simple &
Stylish Patterns
for Dolls' Hats
& Shoes
14" SNEAKER
TONGUE

18"
BASEBALL
CAP SIDE

Simple & Stylish Patterns
for Dolls' Hats & Shoes

14"
SNEAKER
OUTER SOLE

Simple &
Stylish Patterns
for Dolls' Hats
& Shoes

14"
BASEBALL
CAP BILL

Simple & Stylish Patterns
for Dolls' Hats & Shoes

Simple &
Stylish Patterns
for Dolls' Hats
& Shoes
18"
SNEAKER
TONGUE

14"
BASEBALL
CAP SIDE

Simple & Stylish Patterns
for Dolls' Hats & Shoes

9. Turn folded edge of binding to inside of cap and stitch around binding close to fold.

Sneakers

Sizes: To fit 18-inch, 14-inch and 8-inch dolls

Note: Instructions are given for the 18-inch size, with requirements for smaller sizes shown in brackets when applicable. When only one requirement is given, it applies to all three sizes.

Instructions

1. Cut two outer soles each from flannel fabric and craft foam. Trace two sneaker toes, two tongues and two inner soles onto paper side of fusible web; trace four sneaker sides, reversing two. Cut out just outside traced line.

2. Following manufacturer's instructions, fuse toes, tongues and sides onto wrong side of twill fabric; fuse soles onto wrong side of flannel fabric. Cut out on traced lines.

3. Remove paper backing. Fuse bonded twill pieces onto wrong side of flannel fabric; cut out. Fuse bonded soles onto lightweight cardboard; cut out.

4. Trace bonded soles onto paper side of fusible web; cut out. Apply to cardboard side of bonded soles. Remove paper backing; apply to wrong side of flannel outer soles.

5. Sew bias tape over top edges of toes and sides and around top and sides of tongues close to lower edge of binding. Topstitch close to upper edge of binding on sides only.

6. Use zigzag stitch to finish center back edges of sides. Baste front ends of sides over tongue, overlapping slightly at center and having bottom edges even.

7. Position top seam line of toe over seam line of sides; topstitch close to upper edge of binding on toe through all thicknesses.

8. With right sides together, sew center back seams. Press seams open; topstitch over seam allowances. Turn right side out. With air-soluble marker, make a line around bottom edge of sneaker 1/4-inch from raw edge. Finger-press edge under along line.

9. Fold edges of outer sole over inner sole. With sewing needle and matching thread, sew sole to bottom of sneaker along marked line.

10. Glue bottom of sneaker to foam sole; let dry. Trim edges to fit. Using sharp pointed tool, puncture a hole in each sneaker side at point indicated by dot on pattern. Insert laces and tie in a bow.

**8"
BASEBALL
CAP BILL**

Simple & Stylish Patterns
for Dolls' Hats & Shoes

**8"
BASEBALL CAP
SIDE**
Simple & Stylish
Patterns for Dolls'
Hats & Shoes

Simple & Stylish
Patterns for Dolls'
Hats & Shoes

**18"
SNEAKER
OUTER SOLE**

Simple & Stylish
Patterns for Dolls'
Hats & Shoes

**18"
SNEAKER
INNER SOLE**

Simple & Stylish
Patterns for
Dolls' Hats &
Shoes

**14"
SNEAKER
INNER SOLE**

Simple &
Stylish Patterns
for Dolls' Hats
& Shoes

**8"
SNEAKER
INNER
SOLE**

Top edge

Center back

Simple &Stylish Patterns for
Dolls' Hats & Shoes

**18"
SNEAKER SIDE**

Top edge

Center back

Simple &Stylish Patterns
for Dolls' Hats & Shoes

14" SNEAKER SIDE

Top edge

Center back

Simple &Stylish Patterns
for Dolls' Hats & Shoes

8" SNEAKER SIDE

Simple &
Stylish Patterns
for Dolls' Hats
& Shoes

**8"
SNEAKER
OUTER
SOLE**

Top edge

Simple & Stylish Patterns
for Dolls' Hats & Shoes

**18"
SNEAKER TOE**

**8"
SNEAKER
TONGUE**

Beret & Mary Janes

Materials for Beret

- 1/4 yard [1/8 yard for 8-inch size] lightweight wool
- 6 inches [4 inches for 8-inch size] of 1-inch [1/2-inch for 8-inch size] wide ribbon
- 3/4-inch [1/2-inch for 8-inch size] diameter button
- Sewing needle
- Matching thread

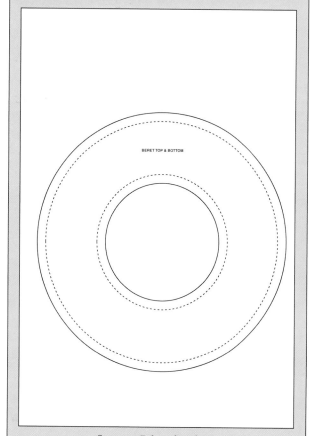

BERET TOP & BOTTOM

See page 7 for color photo.

Materials for Mary Janes

- 1/4 yard [1/8 yard for 8-inch size] black sateen fabric
- 1/4 yard [1/8 yard for 8-inch size] fusible web
- Heavy cardboard
- Cloth carpet tape
- Lightweight cardboard
- Fabric glue
- Seam sealant
- 4 inches [2 inches for 8-inch size] 1/4-inch wide black satin ribbon
- Self-adhesive black hook-and-loop tape
- Two small black buttons or beads
- Fine sewing needle
- Matching thread
- Spring clothespins (optional)

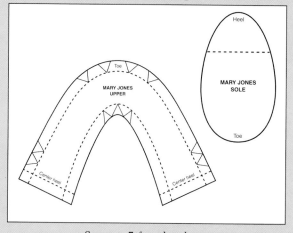

Heel

Toe

MARY JONES SOLE

Toe

MARY JONES UPPER

Center heel

Center heel

See page 7 for color photo.

Beret

Sizes: To fit 18-inch, 14-inch and 8-inch dolls

Note: Instructions are given for the 18-inch size, with requirements for smaller sizes shown in brackets when applicable. When only one requirement is given, it applies to all three sizes.

Pattern Notes

Use 1/4-inch [1/8-inch for 8-inch size] seam allowance throughout unless indicated otherwise.

Set machine stitch size to 10 to 12 stitches per inch.

Clip all seams and curves, as indicated on pattern.

Use zigzag or edging stitch to finish raw edges.

Cutting Instructions

Cut one beret top and bottom from lightweight wool. Cut a 2-inch x 14¾-inch [7¾-inch x 1½-inch for 8-inch size] strip from lightweight wool for band.

Sewing Instructions

1. With right sides together, sew short ends of band together. With wrong sides together, fold band in half.
2. With right sides together, and raw edges even, sew band to edge of bottom. Finish raw edge with zigzag stitch. Press seam toward bottom with right side out.
3. With right sides together, sew top and bottom together around outer edge. Finish seam and turn right side out.
4. Fold ribbon in half. With sewing needle and thread, sew gathering stitch across folded edge of ribbon; pull tightly.
5. Sew gathered edge of ribbon to band over seam. Sew button over gathers. Cut v-notch in each end of ribbon.

Mary Janes

Sizes: To fit 18-inch, 14-inch and 8-inch dolls

Note: Instructions are given for the 18-inch size, with requirements for smaller sizes shown in brackets when applicable. When only one requirement is given, it applies to all three sizes.

Instructions

1. Trace two uppers and two soles on paper side of fusible web. Cut out just outside traced lines. Following manufacturer's instructions, fuse to black sateen fabric. Cut out on traced lines. Remove paper backing. Fuse to lightweight cardboard and cut out.

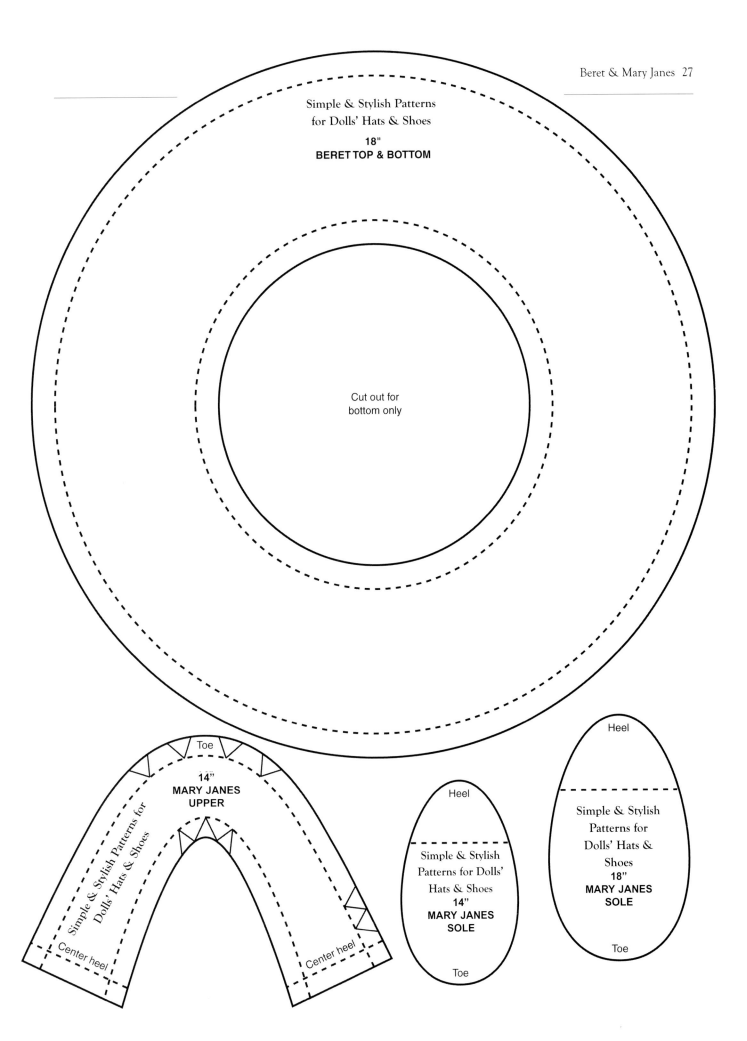

Simple & Stylish Patterns
for Dolls' Hats & Shoes
18"
BERET TOP & BOTTOM

Cut out for
bottom only

Toe

14"
MARY JANES
UPPER

Simple & Stylish Patterns for
Dolls' Hats & Shoes

Center heel

Center heel

Heel

Heel

Simple & Stylish
Patterns for Dolls'
Hats & Shoes
14"
MARY JANES
SOLE

Toe

Simple & Stylish
Patterns for
Dolls' Hats &
Shoes
18"
MARY JANES
SOLE

Toe

2. Cut two uppers from black sateen fabric for facings. With right sides together, sew each facing to one fused-fabric upper. Clip curves; turn right side out. Press. **Note:** *Fabric will bond.*

3. Machine-stitch 1/4-inch [1/8-inch for 8-inch size] from lower edge; clip curves. Finish raw edges with zigzag stitch 1/4-inch [1/8-inch for 8-inch size] from bottom edge of upper. Zigzag heel edges to finish. With right sides together, match raw edges and sew back seam. Turn right side out and press seam open.

4. Apply carpet tape to cardboard sole. Peel paper backing from heel end. With cloth side of sole in shoe, matching centers, and using stitching lines as a guide, fold edge of heel over sole and press.

5. Peel paper from toe end of sole and, matching centers, fold edges over sole and press. Remove paper backing and press remaining edges in place.

6. Apply second piece of carpet tape over folded edges and trim excess. Remove paper backing and apply sole to heavy cardboard. Trim excess.

7. Cut two heels from heavy cardboard. Apply carpet tape to one side; trim away excess. Remove paper backing and adhere heel to bottom of sole.

8. Use black marker to color edges and bottoms of soles and heels.

9. Cut a small piece of hook-and-loop tape equal to width of ribbon. Adhere hook portion to side of shoe and loop portion to end of ribbon.

10. With sewing needle and black thread, sew small button or bead to end of ribbon through tape. Fasten ribbon loop to hook piece on side of shoe. Use fabric glue to tack opposite end of ribbon to inside of shoe, clamping with spring clothespin until set. Let dry.

11. Repeat steps 9 and 10, reversing sides for second shoe.

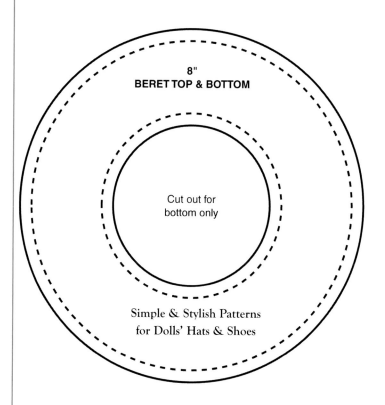

8"
BERET TOP & BOTTOM

Cut out for
bottom only

Simple & Stylish Patterns
for Dolls' Hats & Shoes

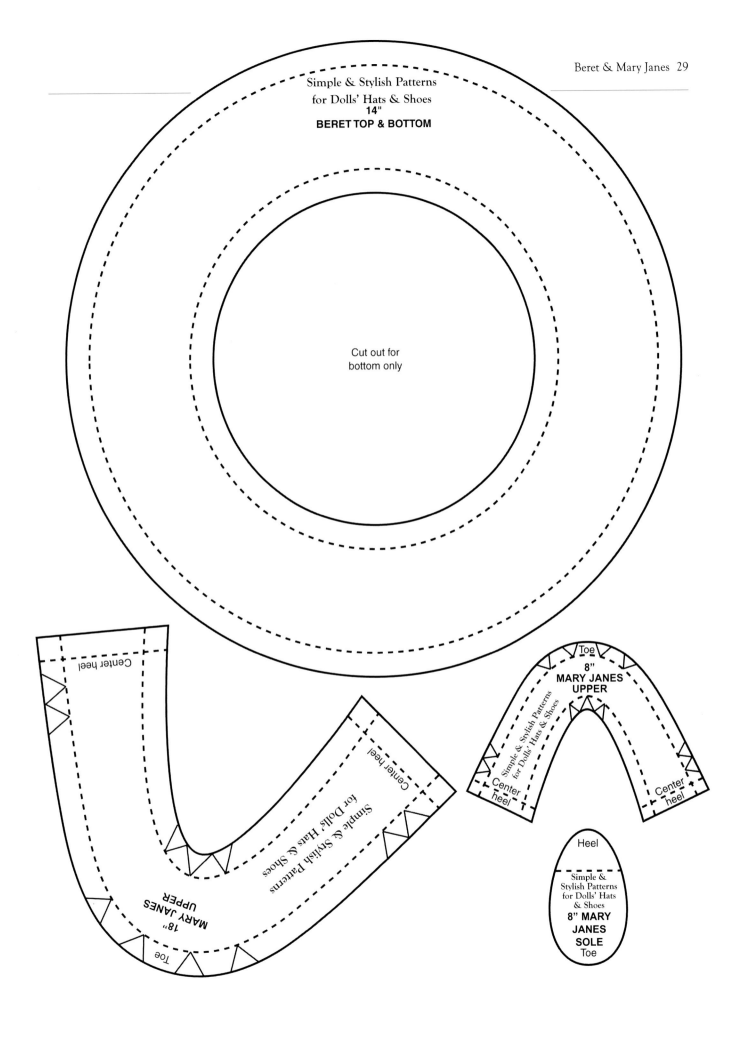

Simple & Stylish Patterns
for Dolls' Hats & Shoes
14"
BERET TOP & BOTTOM

Cut out for
bottom only

Center heel

Center heel

Simple & Stylish Patterns
for Dolls' Hats & Shoes

18" MARY JANES UPPER

Toe

Toe

**8"
MARY JANES
UPPER**

Simple & Stylish Patterns
for Dolls' Hats & Shoes

Center
heel

Center
heel

Heel

Simple &
Stylish Patterns
for Dolls' Hats
& Shoes
**8" MARY
JANES
SOLE**
Toe

Camp Hat & Moccasins

Materials for Camp Hat

- 1/4 yard [1/8 yard for 8-inch size] denim
- 1/4 yard [1/8 yard for 8-inch size] lightweight woven fabric (for lining)
- 1/8 yard suede
- Seed beads
- Sewing needle (fine)
- One silver shank-back button

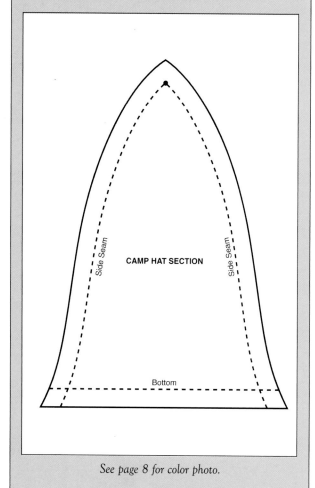

See page 8 for color photo.

Materials for Moccasins

- 1/8 yard suede or synthetic suede
- Ten seed beads
- Needle (fine)
- White thread
- Fabric glue
- Two spring clothespins

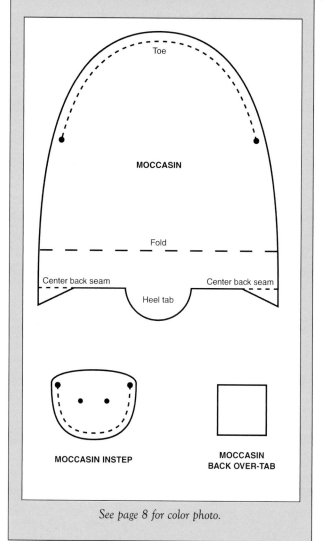

See page 8 for color photo.

Camp Hat

Sizes: To fit 18-inch, 14-inch and 8-inch dolls

Note: Instructions are given for the 18-inch size, with requirements for smaller sizes shown in brackets when applicable. When only one requirement is given, it applies to all three sizes.

Pattern Notes

Use 1/4-inch [1/8-inch for 8-inch size] seam allowance throughout unless indicated otherwise.

Set machine stitch size to 10–12 stitches per inch.

Clip all seams and curves, as indicated on pattern.

Use zigzag or edging stitch to finish raw edges.

Cutting Instructions

1. Cut six hat sections from denim and six hat sections from lightweight woven fabric.
2. Cut emblem from suede.

Sewing Instructions

1. With right sides together, sew hat sections together along side seams. Press seams.
2. With right sides together, sew lining sections together. Press seams.
3. With right sides together, sew hat and lining together along bottom edge leaving one to two inches open for turning.
4. Turn lining inside hat. Press seam. Topstitch around bottom edge.

Finishing Instructions

1. Thread needle with double strand of thread and knot ends.
2. Bring needle from back to front through suede emblem at any center dot. Thread three seed beads and bring needle from top to bottom through corresponding outer dot. Make small stitch on wrong side to secure back through next center dot and repeat. Knot thread on wrong side. Length of beaded strands may vary.
3. Sew small stitch on wrong side to secure. Repeat around entire emblem. Tie knot on wrong side to secure.
   Note: *Use dots as guide only.*

Moccasins

Sizes: To fit 18-inch, 14-inch and 8-inch dolls

Note: Instructions are given for the 18-inch size, with requirements for smaller sizes shown in brackets when applicable. When only one requirement is given, it applies to all three sizes.

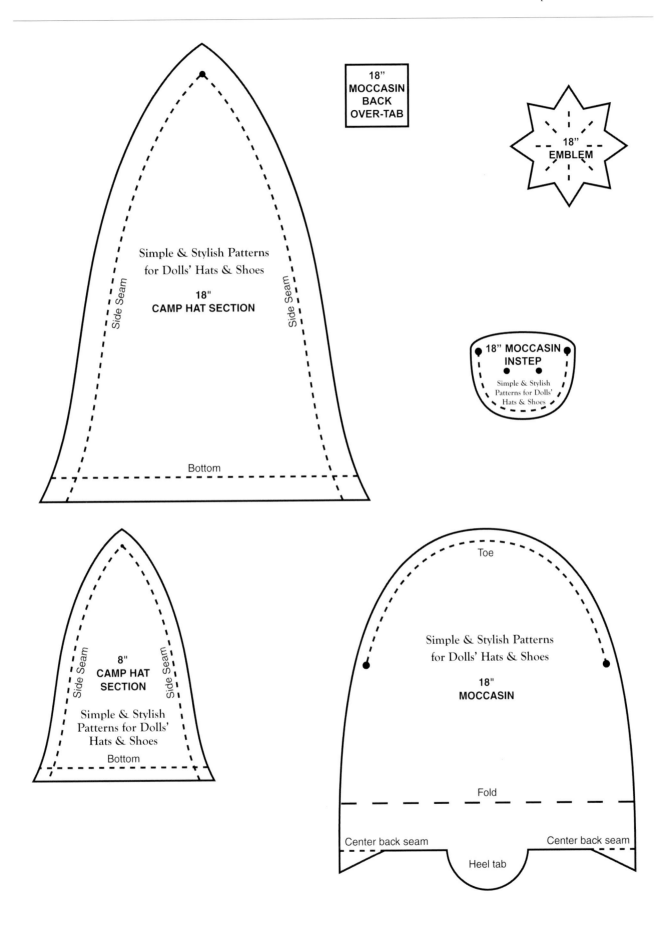

18"
MOCCASIN
BACK
OVER-TAB

18"
EMBLEM

Side Seam

Side Seam

Simple & Stylish Patterns
for Dolls' Hats & Shoes

**18"
CAMP HAT SECTION**

Bottom

18" MOCCASIN
INSTEP

Simple & Stylish
Patterns for Dolls'
Hats & Shoes

Side Seam

Side Seam

**8"
CAMP HAT
SECTION**

Simple & Stylish
Patterns for Dolls'
Hats & Shoes

Bottom

Toe

Simple & Stylish Patterns
for Dolls' Hats & Shoes

**18"
MOCCASIN**

Fold

Center back seam

Center back seam

Heel tab

1. Cut two moccasins, two tabs and two insteps from suede or synthetic suede.

2. With needle and thread, sew gathering stitches on toes of each moccasin, as indicated on pattern.

3. Place moccasin over instep and pull gathering stitch to match moccasin to instep piece. Knot thread.

4. With right sides together, sew center back seams. Open seams and stitch across top to hold.

5. Apply fabric glue to each heel tab. Fold up to form heel. Clamp with clothespin and let dry.

6. Place tab over center back seam and stitch or glue in place.

7. Thread needle with double strand of thread. Knot ends. Bring needle from wrong side of moccasin at dots.

8. Thread five seed beads on needle and sew to moccasin by bringing needle through to wrong side at opposite dot. Repeat for second moccasin. Knot on wrong side.

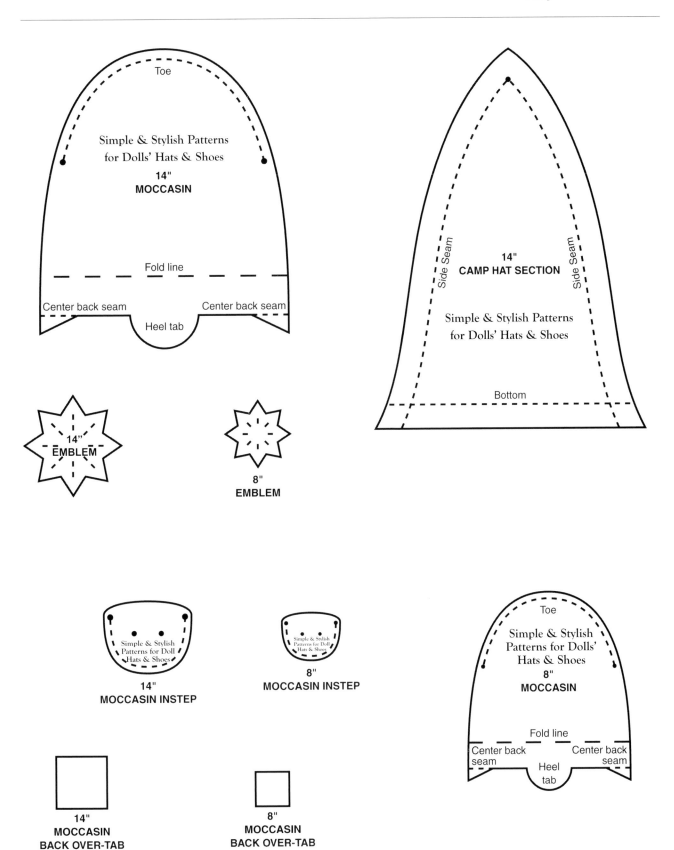

Toe

Simple & Stylish Patterns
for Dolls' Hats & Shoes
14"
MOCCASIN

Fold line

Center back seam   Center back seam

Heel tab

14"
CAMP HAT SECTION

Side Seam   Side Seam

Simple & Stylish Patterns
for Dolls' Hats & Shoes

Bottom

14"
EMBLEM

8"
EMBLEM

Simple & Stylish
Patterns for Doll
Hats & Shoes

14"
MOCCASIN INSTEP

Simple & Stylish
Patterns for Doll
Hats & Shoes

8"
MOCCASIN INSTEP

Toe

Simple & Stylish
Patterns for Dolls'
Hats & Shoes
8"
MOCCASIN

Fold line

Center back
seam   Center back
seam

Heel
tab

14"
MOCCASIN
BACK OVER-TAB

8"
MOCCASIN
BACK OVER-TAB

Communion Veil & T-Strap Shoes

Materials for Communion Veil

- 1/4 yard white patterned tulle netting
- Two 3/8-inch metal hair clips
- White satin floral spray with pearls
- Hot-glue gun and glue sticks
- Sewing needle
- White heavy-duty thread

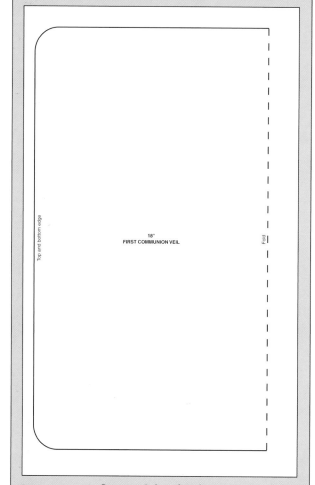

See page 9 for color photo.

Materials for T-Strap Shoes

- 1/8 yard white satin fabric
- 9½ inches of 1/4-inch [4 inches of 1/8-inch for 8-inch size] wide white satin picot-edged ribbon
- Needle (fine)
- White thread
- Two snaps
- Lightweight cardboard
- Heavyweight cardboard
- Cloth carpet tape
- 1/8 yard fusible web
- Black permanent marker

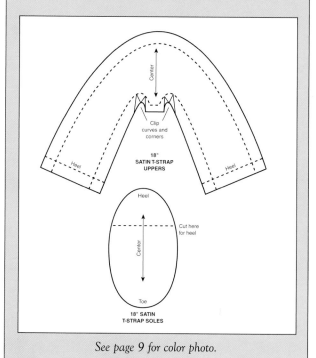

See page 9 for color photo.

Communion Veil

Sizes: To fit 18-inch, 14-inch and 8-inch dolls

Note: Instructions are given for the 18-inch size, with requirements for smaller sizes shown in brackets when applicable. When only one requirement is given, it applies to all three sizes.

Pattern Notes

Use 1/4-inch [1/8-inch for 8-inch size] seam allowance throughout unless indicated otherwise.

Set machine stitch size to 10–12 stitches per inch.

Clip all seams and curves, as indicated on pattern.

Use zigzag or edging stitch to finish raw edges.

Cutting Instructions

Cut two veils from tulle.

Sewing Instructions

1. Fold top edge of one veil piece over 1/4 inch and machine-gather close to fold. Pull gathers to fit clip.
2. Fold top edge of second veil 1 inch and machine-gather close to fold. Pull gathers to fit clip.
3. Sew gathered edges together.
4. With needle and doubled heavy-duty thread, stitch gathered edges to top of hair clip.
5. Separate floral spray. Trim wire stems.
6. Hot-glue leaves, flowers and pearl sprays to gathered edges of tulle.

T-Strap Shoes

Sizes: To fit 18-inch, 14-inch and 8-inch dolls

Note: Instructions are given for the 18-inch size, with requirements for smaller sizes shown in brackets when applicable. When only one requirement is given, it applies to all three sizes.

Instructions

1. Trace two uppers and two soles on paper side of fusible web and cut out just outside traced lines. Following manufacturer's instructions, fuse with white satin fabric; cut out on traced lines. Remove paper backing. Fuse soles to lightweight cardboard; trim excess cardboard.
2. Cut two uppers from white satin. Cut two 1½ inches [3/4-inch for 8-inch size] lengths of ribbon. Fold in half. Place folded ribbon on satin upper with ends extending toward heel and folded edge toward toe. With 3/8-inch [1/8-inch for 8-inch size] loop on folded

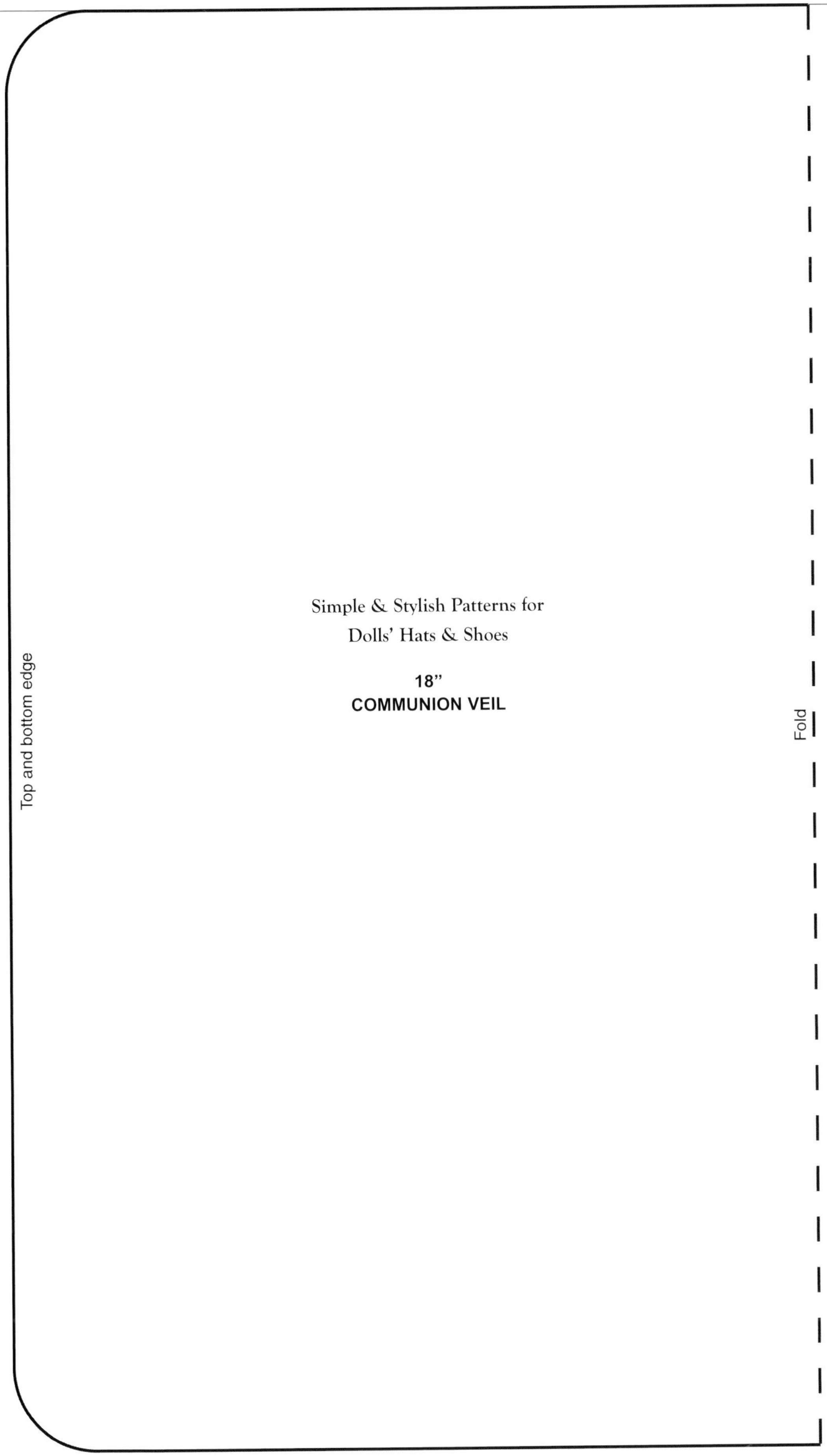

Top and bottom edge

Simple & Stylish Patterns for
Dolls' Hats & Shoes

18"
COMMUNION VEIL

Fold

edge extending past seam line, baste.

3. With right sides together, sew bonded uppers to satin uppers along inner edges. Turn right side out. Clip curves and trim corners. Turn right side out. Press. **Note:** *Fabric will bond.*

4. Sew zigzag stitch to finish heel edges. With right sides together, sew heel seams. Press open and stitch across top edge.

5. Apply carpet tape to cardboard sole. Peel paper backing from heel end. With white satin side of sole in shoe, matching centers and using stitching lines as a guide, fold edge of heel over sole and press.

6. Peel paper from toe end of sole and, matching centers, fold edges over sole and press. Remove paper backing and press remaining edges in place.

7. Apply second piece of carpet tape over folded edges and trim excess. Remove paper backing and apply sole to heavy cardboard. Trim excess.

8. Cut two heels from heavy cardboard. Apply carpet tape to one side, trim away excess. Remove paper backing and adhere heel to bottom of sole.

Finishing Instructions

1. Cut remaining ribbon in half. Fold

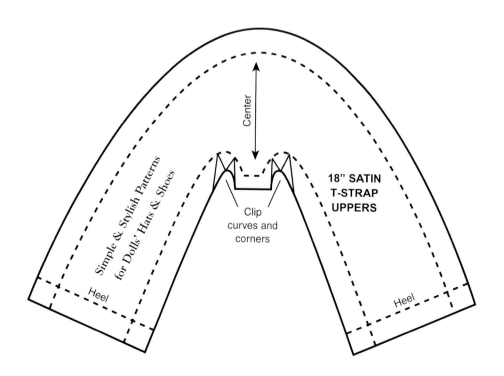

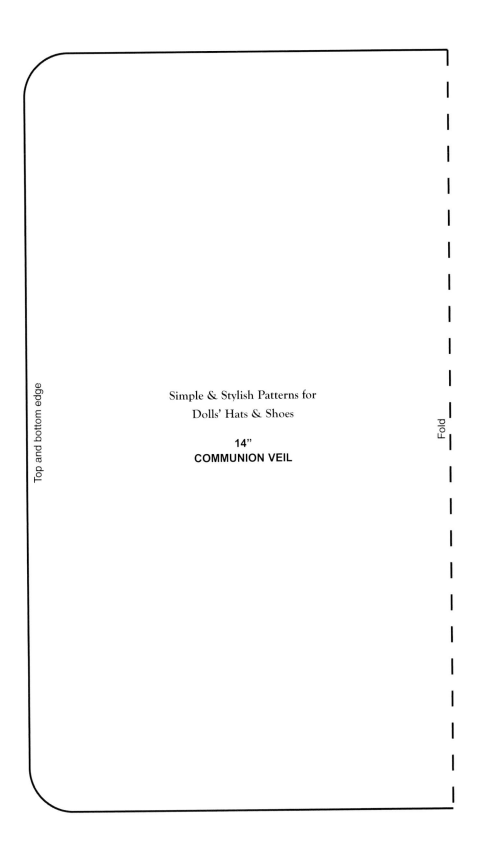

Top and bottom edge

Simple & Stylish Patterns for
Dolls' Hats & Shoes

14"
COMMUNION VEIL

Fold

one end under 1/4-inch [1/8-inch for 8-inch size] twice. Tack in place. Sew snap to upper and folded end of ribbon as indicated on pattern.

2. Insert opposite ribbon end through ribbon loop on upper center. Tack end inside upper at point indicated on pattern. Trim excess.

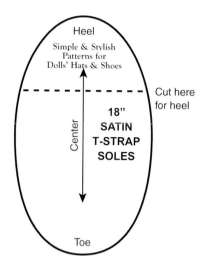

Heel

Simple & Stylish Patterns for Dolls' Hats & Shoes

Cut here for heel

Center

18" SATIN T-STRAP SOLES

Toe

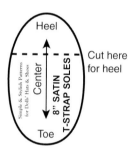

Heel

Cut here for heel

Center

Simple & Stylish Patterns for Dolls' Hats & Shoes

8" SATIN T-STRAP SOLES

Toe

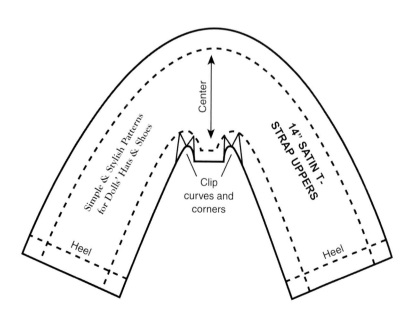

Center

Simple & Stylish Patterns for Dolls' Hats & Shoes

14" SATIN T-STRAP UPPERS

Clip curves and corners

Heel

Heel

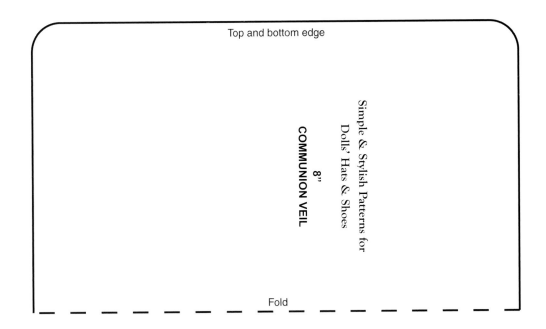

Top and bottom edge

8"
COMMUNION VEIL

Simple & Stylish Patterns for
Dolls' Hats & Shoes

Fold

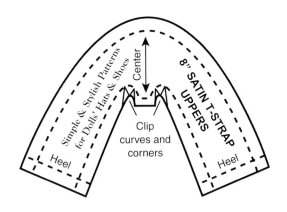

Center

8" SATIN T-STRAP
UPPERS

Simple & Stylish Patterns
for Dolls' Hats & Shoes

Clip
curves and
corners

Heel

Heel

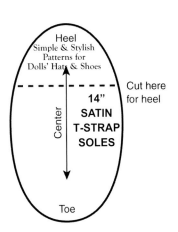

Heel
Simple & Stylish
Patterns for
Dolls' Hats & Shoes

Cut here
for heel

14"
SATIN
T-STRAP
SOLES

Center

Toe

Dainty Spring Bonnet & Mary Janes

Materials for Dainty Spring Bonnet

- 15-inch [8-inch for 8-inch size] diameter lace doily
- Satin ribbon rose garland with 14 roses [11 roses for 8-inch size]
- 4- to 5-inch [2- to 2½-inch for 8-inch size] plastic foam ball
- Plastic wrap
- Straight pins
- Waxed paper
- Fabric stiffener
- Paintbrush
- Fabric glue

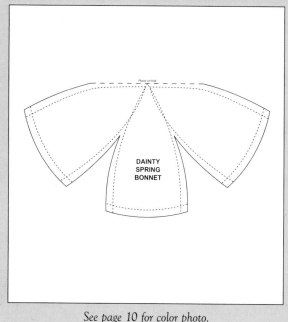

See page 10 for color photo.

Materials for Mary Janes

- 1/4 yard [1/8 yard for 8-inch size] black satin fabric
- 1/4 yard [1/8 yard for 8-inch size] fusible web
- Heavy cardboard
- Cloth carpet tape
- Lightweight cardboard
- Fabric glue
- Seam sealant
- 4 inches [2 inches for 8-inch size] 1/4-inch wide black satin ribbon
- Self-adhesive black hook-and-loop tape
- Two small buttons or beads (gold is used on the 8-inch size)
- Fine sewing needle
- Matching thread
- Spring clothespins (optional)

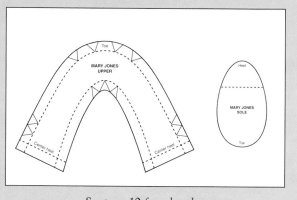

See page 10 for color photo.

Dainty Spring Bonnet

Sizes: To fit 18-inch, 14-inch and 8-inch dolls

Note: Instructions are given for the 18-inch size, with requirements for smaller sizes shown in brackets when applicable. When only one requirement is given, it applies to all three sizes.

Pattern Notes

Use 1/4-inch [1/8-inch for 8-inch size] seam allowance throughout unless indicated otherwise.

Set machine stitch size to 10–12 stitches per inch.

Clip all seams and curves, as indicated on pattern.

Use zigzag or edging stitch to finish raw edges.

Instructions

1. With right sides together, fold doily in half. Place hat pattern on fold and cut out, leaving scalloped edge of doily.
2. For brim, cut away excess of doily from outer edge so scalloped edge measures 1½ inches [1 inch for 8-inch size] wide.
3. Sew across top edge of hat, as indicated on pattern. Open hat and refold so raw edges of next two sections meet across top. Restitch in same manner.
4. Trim seams evenly and finish edges with zigzag stitch. Turn hat right side out.
5. Open scalloped edge of doily. With sewing machine, gather doily 1/4 inch [1/8 inch for 8-inch size] from inside raw edge. Pull gathers to fit bottom edge of hat.
6. With right sides together and raw edges even, sew brim to bottom edge of hat. Trim seam evenly and finish with zigzag stitch.
7. Cover plastic foam ball with plastic wrap. To keep stationary, place in cup or other container. Place hat on ball and apply fabric stiffener with paint brush. Let dry. Remove from ball.
8. Glue satin ribbon rose garland around hat just above brim.

Mary Janes

Sizes: To fit 18-inch, 14-inch and 8-inch dolls

Note: Instructions are given for the 18-inch size, with requirements for smaller sizes shown in brackets when applicable. When only one requirement is given, it applies to all three sizes.

Instructions

1. Trace two uppers and two soles on paper side of fusible web. Cut out just outside traced lines. Following manu- facturer's instructions, fuse to black

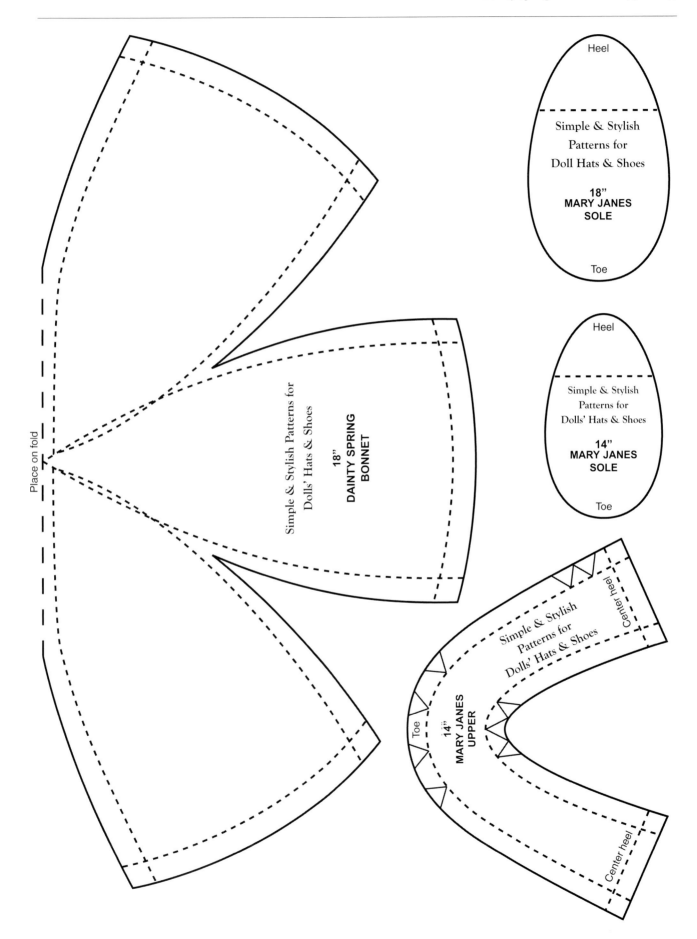

Heel

Simple & Stylish
Patterns for
Doll Hats & Shoes

**18"
MARY JANES
SOLE**

Toe

Heel

Simple & Stylish
Patterns for
Dolls' Hats & Shoes

**14"
MARY JANES
SOLE**

Toe

Place on fold

Simple & Stylish Patterns for
Dolls' Hats & Shoes

**18"
DAINTY SPRING
BONNET**

Simple & Stylish
Patterns for
Dolls' Hats & Shoes

**14"
MARY JANES
UPPER**

Toe

Center heel

Center heel

satin fabric. Cut out on traced lines. Remove paper backing. Fuse to light-weight cardboard and cut out.

2. Cut two uppers from black satin fabric for facings. With right sides together, sew each facing to one fused-fabric upper. Clip curves; turn right side out. Press. **Note**: *Fabric will bond.*

3. Machine-stitch 1/4 inch [1/8 inch for 8-inch size] from lower edge; clip curves. Finish raw edges with zigzag stitch 1/4 inch [1/8 inch for 8-inch size] from bottom edge of upper. Zigzag heel edges to finish. With right sides together, match raw edges and sew back seam. Turn right side out and press seam open.

4. Apply carpet tape to cardboard sole. Peel paper backing from heel end. With cloth side of sole in shoe, matching centers, and using stitching lines as a guide, fold edge of heel over sole and press.

5. Peel paper from toe end of sole and, matching centers, fold edges over sole and press. Remove paper backing and press remaining edges in place.

6. Apply second piece of carpet tape over folded edges and trim excess. Remove paper backing and apply sole to heavy cardboard. Trim excess.

7. Cut two heels from heavy cardboard. Apply carpet tape to one side; trim away excess. Remove paper backing and adhere heel to bottom of sole.

8. Use black marker to color edges and bottoms of soles and heels.

9. Cut a small piece of hook-and-loop tape equal to width of ribbon. Adhere hook portion to side of shoe and loop portion to end of ribbon.

10. With sewing needle and black thread, sew small button or bead to end of ribbon through tape. Fasten ribbon loop to hook piece on side of shoe. Use fabric glue to tack opposite end of ribbon to inside of shoe, clamping with spring clothespin until set. Let dry.

11. Repeat steps 9 and 10, reversing sides for second shoe.

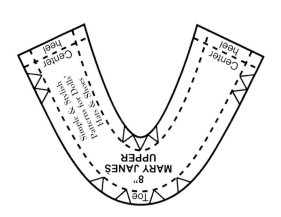

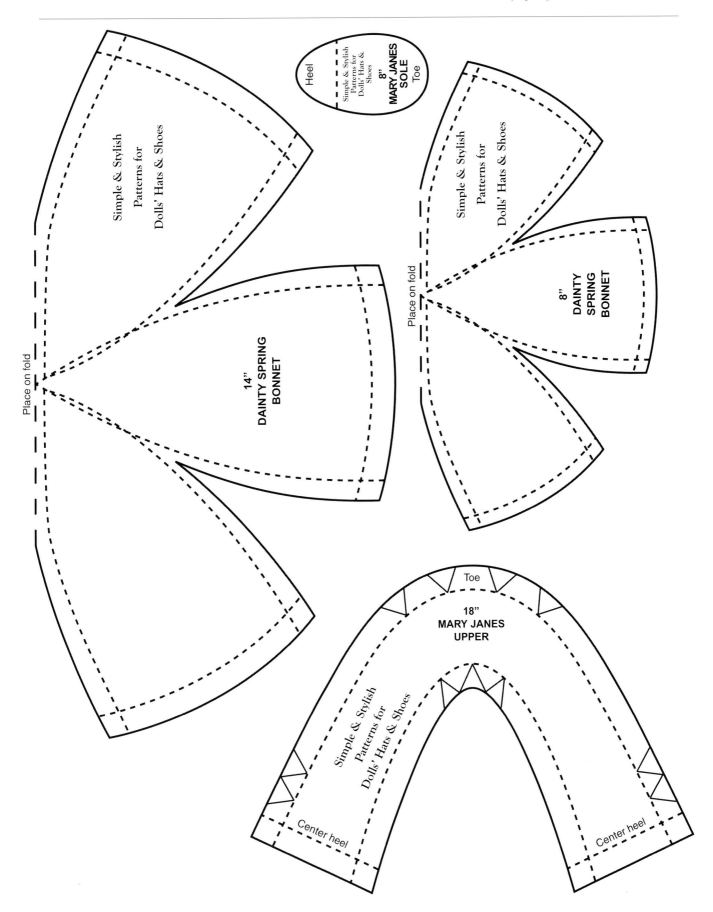

Heel

Simple & Stylish
Patterns for
Dolls' Hats &
Shoes

8"
MARY JANES
SOLE

Toe

Simple & Stylish
Patterns for
Dolls' Hats & Shoes

Simple & Stylish
Patterns for
Dolls' Hats & Shoes

8"
DAINTY
SPRING
BONNET

Place on fold

Place on fold

14"
DAINTY SPRING
BONNET

Toe

18"
MARY JANES
UPPER

Simple & Stylish
Patterns for
Dolls' Hats & Shoes

Center heel

Center heel

Feathered Headpiece & Ballet Slippers

Materials for Feathered Headpiece

- 13-inch x 7-1/8-inch piece of pink satin fabric
- Two small decorative feathers
- Earring or fancy shank-back button
- Seam sealant (optional)
- Hot-glue gun and glue sticks
- Fabric glue
- Wire cutters

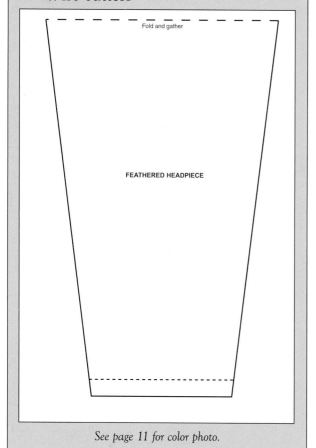

See page 11 for color photo.

Materials for Ballet Slippers

- 1/4 yard [1/8 yard for 8-inch size] pink satin fabric
- Cloth carpet tape
- 18 inches of 1/4-inch [12 inches of 1/8-inch for 8-inch size] wide pink ribbon
- Small piece lightweight cardboard
- Seam sealant
- 1/4 yard [1/8 yard for 8-inch size] fusible web
- Sewing needle
- Matching thread
- Small amount polyester fiberfill (optional)

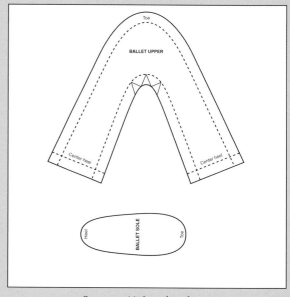

See page 11 for color photo.

Feathered Headpiece

Sizes: To fit 18-inch, 14-inch and 8-inch dolls

Note: Instructions are given for the 18-inch size, with requirements for smaller sizes shown in brackets when applicable. When only one requirement is given, it applies to all three sizes.

Pattern Notes

Use 1/4-inch [1/8-inch for 8-inch size] seam allowance throughout unless indicated otherwise.

Set machine stitch size to 10–12 stitches per inch.

Clip all seams and curves, as indicated on pattern.

Use zigzag or edging stitch to finish raw edges.

Instructions

1. Press under long edges of satin fabric. With sewing machine, sew a gathering stitch down center of fabric (Fig. 1). Pull gathers tightly and knot threads securely at both ends.
2. Tie threads together on both ends on wrong side. Trim thread close to knots. Secure knot with drop of seam sealant, if desired.
3. With right sides together, sew short edges together using a gathering stitch. Pull stitches tightly together. Trim seam evenly and use zigzag stitch to finish raw edges. Turn right side out.
4. Glue ends of decorative feathers over center front gathers using hot glue. Using wire cutters, snip off earring back or button shank. Glue earring or button over ends of feathers.

Ballet Slippers

Sizes: To fit 18-inch, 14-inch and 8-inch dolls

Note: Instructions are given for the 18-inch size, with requirements for smaller sizes shown in brackets when applicable. When only one requirement is given, it applies to all three sizes.

Instructions

1. Cut four uppers and four soles from pink satin fabric. Sew two uppers together with right sides together along inner seam. Clip curves. Apply seam sealant to edges of two soles.
2. Turn uppers right side out; press. Open uppers; hold, with right sides together, matching center heel seams; sew seam across both uppers; press seam open. Fold one upper inside the other for liner.

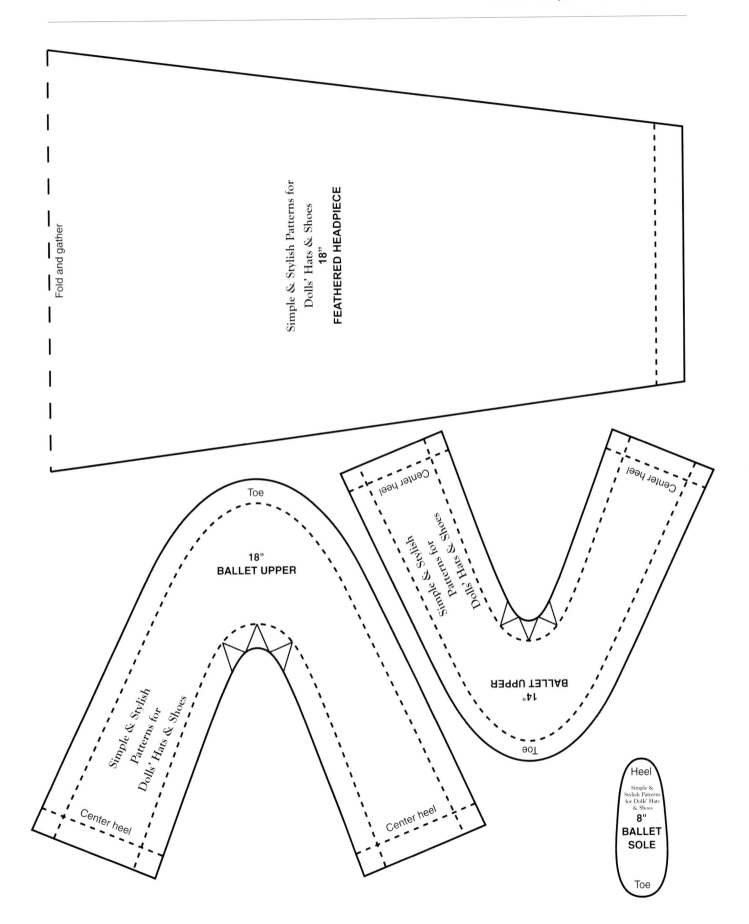

Fold and gather

Simple & Stylish Patterns for
Dolls' Hats & Shoes
18"
FEATHERED HEADPIECE

Toe

18"
BALLET UPPER

Simple & Stylish
Patterns for
Dolls' Hats & Shoes

Center heel

Center heel

Center heel

Center heel

Simple & Stylish
Patterns for
Dolls' Hats & Shoes

14"
BALLET UPPER

Toe

Heel

Simple &
Stylish Patterns
for Dolls' Hats
& Shoes
8"
**BALLET
SOLE**

Toe

3. Following manufacturer's instructions, fuse two soles to a lightweight piece of cardboard. Adhere a length of cloth carpet tape to cardboard side of soles to cover; trim away excess.

4. With sewing machine, make a gathering stitch 1/4 inch [1/8 inch for 8-inch size] from lower edges. Pull to gather to fit around fused sole; adjust gathers around toe.

5. Peel tape backing from heel end of sole. With fabric side of sole on inside of upper, using stitching line as a guide and, matching centers, fold heel edge of upper over sole and adhere to tape.

6. Peel tape backing from toe end of sole; fold toe edge of upper over sole and adhere to tape. Remove remaining tape backing and press edges of upper to sole all around.

7. Adhere wrong side of remaining satin soles to carpet tape; trim away excess tape. Apply to bottoms of soles, covering folded edges.

8. Thread sewing needle with a doubled length of thread; knot ends. Insert needle from inside slipper at center back seam approximately 1/4 inch [1/8 inch for 8-inch size] from top edge. Bring needle back through slipper close to top edge. Knot thread to secure, leaving a very small amount of slack in loop on back of slipper. Bring needle back through slipper at same point to come out at end of loop just made. Referring to Fig. 2, work buttonhole stitch across thread loop; knot thread on inside of slipper to secure and trim close to knot. Apply a dot of seam sealant to knot, if desired.

9. Cut ribbon in half. Center each half over slipper at point indicated on pattern and tack to sides of slipper. Place slipper on doll. Cross ribbons over foot in front of ankle, wrap around ankle and insert both ends from opposite sides through buttonhole loop on back of slipper. Crisscross around leg as desired. Tie ends in bow at front.

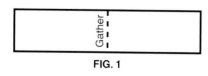

FIG. 1

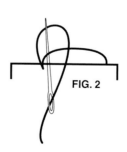

FIG. 2

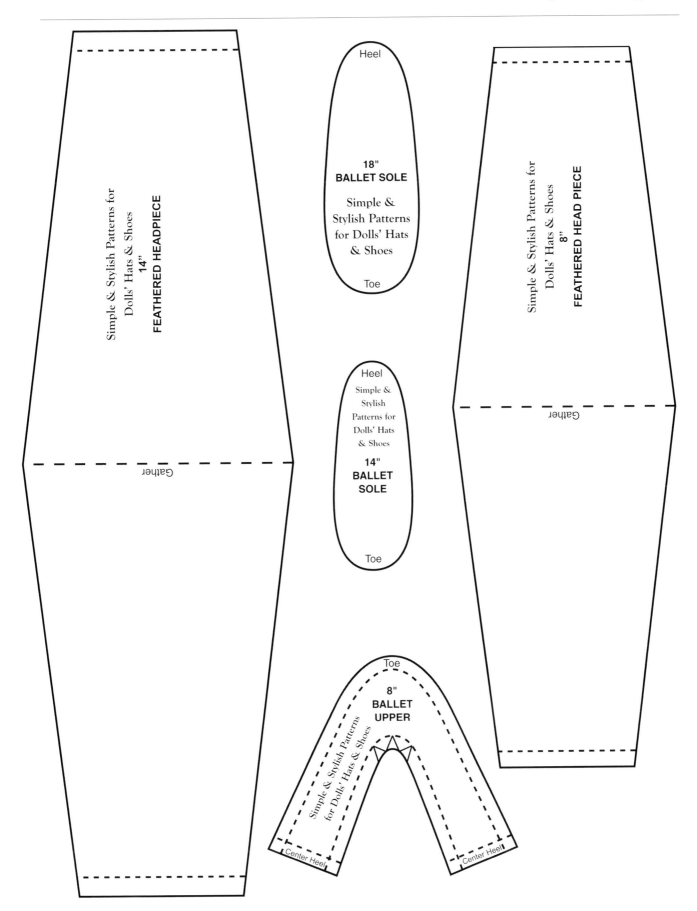

Simple & Stylish Patterns for
Dolls' Hats & Shoes
14"
FEATHERED HEADPIECE

Gather

Heel

18"
BALLET SOLE

Simple &
Stylish Patterns
for Dolls' Hats
& Shoes

Toe

Heel

Simple &
Stylish
Patterns for
Dolls' Hats
& Shoes

14"
BALLET
SOLE

Toe

Simple & Stylish Patterns for
Dolls' Hats & Shoes
8"
FEATHERED HEAD PIECE

Gather

Toe

8"
BALLET
UPPER

Simple & Stylish Patterns
for Dolls' Hats & Shoes

Center Heel

Center Heel

Fleece Hat & Oxfords

Materials for Fleece Hat

- 1/4 yard [1/8 yard for 8-inch size] fleece fabric
- 12 inches grosgrain ribbon or cording [for 8-inch size]

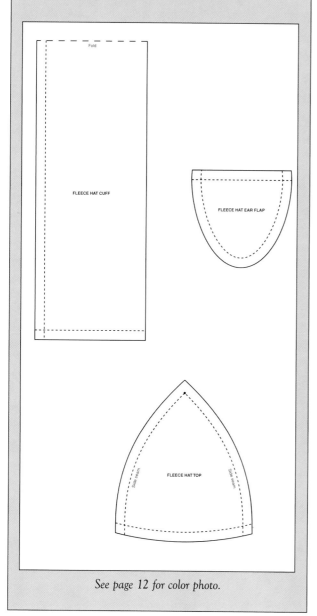

See page 12 for color photo.

Materials for Oxfords

- 1/8 yard vinyl
- 1/8 yard flannel
- Lightweight cardboard
- Heavy cardboard
- Cloth carpet tape
- Awl
- 18 inches [12 inches for 8-inch size] narrow cording (for laces)
- 1/8 yard fusible web
- Black permanent marker
- Transparent tape

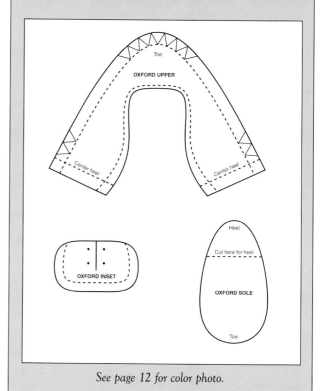

See page 12 for color photo.

Fleece Hat

Sizes: To fit 18-inch, 14-inch and 8-inch dolls

Note: Instructions are given for the 18-inch size, with requirements for smaller sizes shown in brackets when applicable. When only one requirement is given, it applies to all three sizes.

Pattern Notes

Use 1/4-inch [1/8-inch for 8-inch size] seam allowance throughout unless indicated otherwise.

Set machine stitch size to 10–12 stitches per inch.

Clip all seams and curves, as indicated on pattern.

Cutting Instructions

From fleece fabric, cut four hat tops, four ear flaps and one hat cuff (on fold) and one 17-inch x 1½-inch piece for ties [cording will be used for ties on the 8-inch size].

Sewing Instructions

1. With right sides together, sew two ear flaps together. Repeat for other flap.
2. With right side of hat cuff and wrong side of hat together, and with ear flap sandwiched between cuff and hat, sew cuff to bottom edge of cap.
3. Fold seam allowance over right side of hat and topstitch. Fold raw edge of cuff to seam; hand-stitch in place.
4. Fold 17-inch x 1½-inch piece in half lengthwise. With right sides together, sew along long edge. Turn right side out. [For 8-inch size, fold 12-inch piece of grosgrain ribbon or cording in half.]
5. Cut in two equal pieces. Pin each tie to inside of earflap, 1/4 inch from bottom inside edge.
6. Sew, using zigzag stitch. Repeat for second tie. Knot ends of ties.

Oxfords

Sizes: To fit 18-inch, 14-inch and 8-inch dolls

Note: Instructions are given for the 18-inch size, with requirements for smaller sizes shown in brackets when applicable. When only one requirement is given, it applies to all three sizes.

Instructions

1. Cut two uppers and two insets from vinyl. Trace two soles on paper side of fusible web. Following manufacturer's instructions, fuse to flannel and cut two soles.
2. Fuse bonded flannel soles to light-weight cardboard; cut out.
3. Place oxford upper over inset, matching

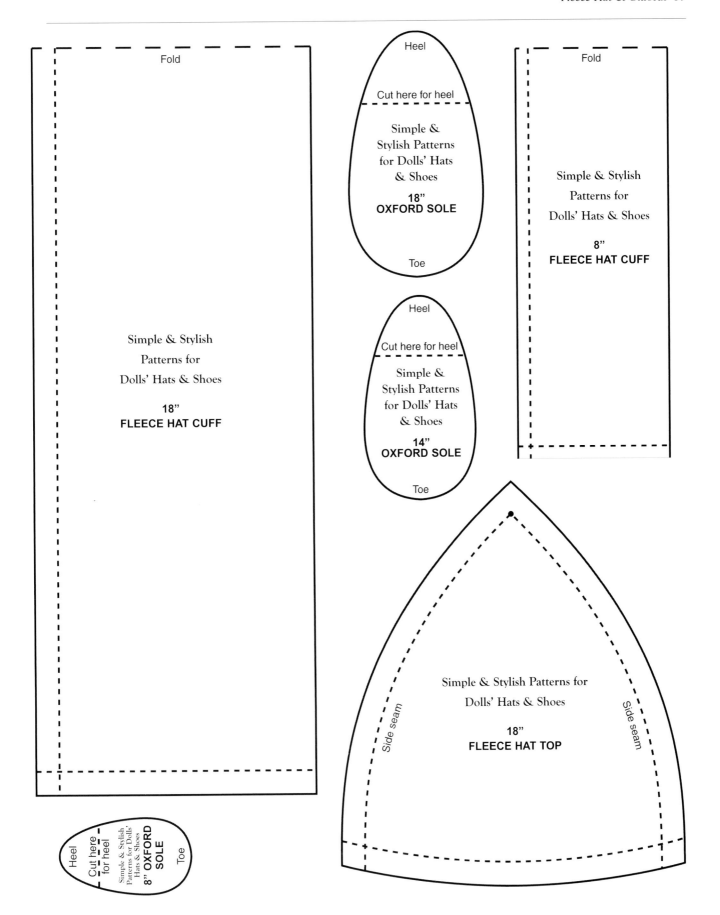

Fold

Heel

Cut here for heel

Simple &
Stylish Patterns
for Dolls' Hats
& Shoes
**18"
OXFORD SOLE**

Toe

Fold

Simple & Stylish
Patterns for
Dolls' Hats & Shoes

**8"
FLEECE HAT CUFF**

Simple & Stylish
Patterns for
Dolls' Hats & Shoes

**18"
FLEECE HAT CUFF**

Heel

Cut here for heel

Simple &
Stylish Patterns
for Dolls' Hats
& Shoes
**14"
OXFORD SOLE**

Toe

Side seam

Simple & Stylish Patterns for
Dolls' Hats & Shoes

**18"
FLEECE HAT TOP**

Side seam

Heel

Cut here
for heel

Simple & Stylish
Patterns for Dolls'
Hats & Shoes
**8" OXFORD
SOLE**

Toe

seam lines. Machine-stitch 1/4 inch from bottom edge. Machine-stitch over back edges with zigzag stitch to finish. Sew center back seam. Open seam and stitch across back edge.

4. Apply carpet tape to cardboard sole. Peel paper backing from heel end. With flannel side of sole in shoe, matching centers, and using stitching lines as a guide, fold edge of heel over sole and press.

5. Peel paper from toe end of sole and, matching centers, fold edges over sole and press. Remove paper backing and press remaining edges in place.

6. Apply second piece of carpet tape over folded edges and trim excess. Remove paper backing and apply sole to heavy cardboard. Trim excess.

7. Cut two heels from heavy cardboard. Apply carpet tape to one side; trim

away excess. Remove paper backing and adhere heel to bottom of sole.

8. Use black marker to color edges and bottoms of soles and heels.

9. As indicated on pattern, cut crisscross slits in inset. Cut cording in half. Wrap transparent tape around each end of cording. Insert wrapped ends through slits for laces. Tie in bows.

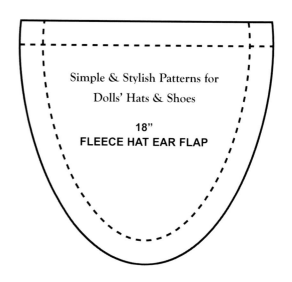

Simple & Stylish Patterns for
Dolls' Hats & Shoes

18"
FLEECE HAT EAR FLAP

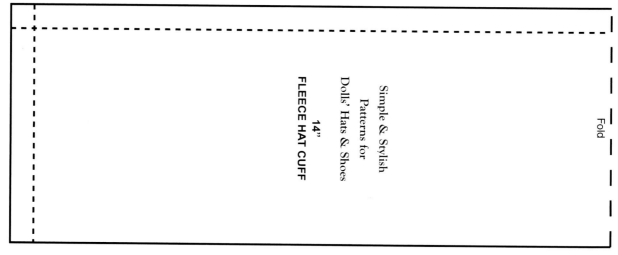

14"
FLEECE HAT CUFF

Simple & Stylish
Patterns for
Dolls' Hats & Shoes

Fold

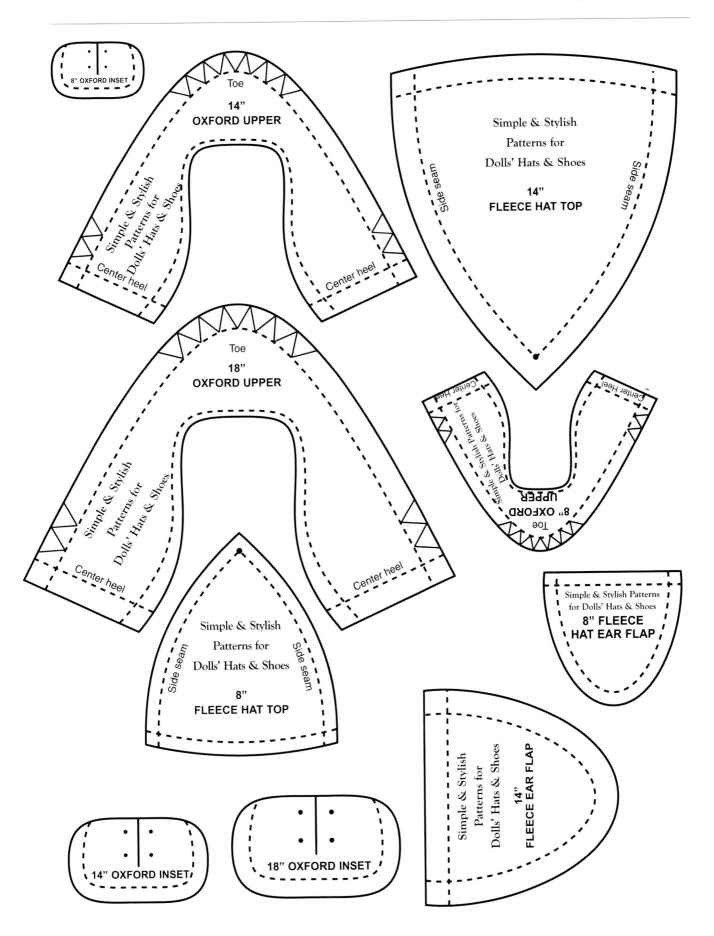

8" OXFORD INSET

Toe
14"
OXFORD UPPER

Simple & Stylish Patterns for Dolls' Hats & Shoes

Center heel

Center heel

Simple & Stylish
Patterns for
Dolls' Hats & Shoes
14"
FLEECE HAT TOP

Side seam

Side seam

Toe
18"
OXFORD UPPER

Simple & Stylish
Patterns for
Dolls' Hats & Shoes

Center heel

Center heel

Center Heel

Center Heel

Toe
8" OXFORD
UPPER

Simple & Stylish Patterns for
Dolls' Hats & Shoes

Simple & Stylish
Patterns for
Dolls' Hats & Shoes
8"
FLEECE HAT TOP

Side seam

Side seam

Simple & Stylish Patterns
for Dolls' Hats & Shoes
8" FLEECE
HAT EAR FLAP

Simple & Stylish
Patterns for
Dolls' Hats & Shoes
14"
FLEECE EAR FLAP

14" OXFORD INSET

18" OXFORD INSET

Rain Hat & Puddle Jumpers

Materials for Rain Hat

- 3/8 yard [1/4 yard for 8-inch size] vinyl with bonded lining
- 3/8 yard [1/4 yard for 8-inch size] black double-folded bias binding
- One 5/8-inch [1/2-inch for 8-inch size] black shank-back button

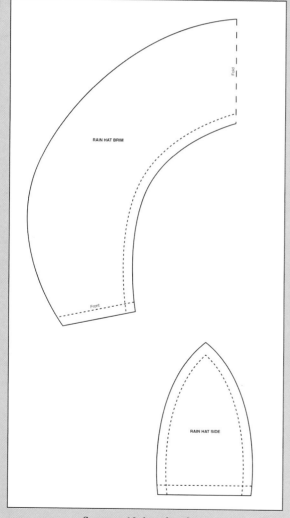

See page 13 for color photo.

Materials for Puddle Jumpers

- 1/4 yard [1/8 yard for 8-inch size] vinyl with bonded lining
- Four one-inch [1/2-inch for 8-inch size] pieces of 5/8-inch [1/4-inch for 8-inch size] wide elastic
- Craft foam (black)
- Carpet tape
- Lightweight cardboard
- Fabric glue
- Seam sealant
- Cloth carpet tape
- 6 inches [3 inches for 8-inch size] black double-fold bias tape

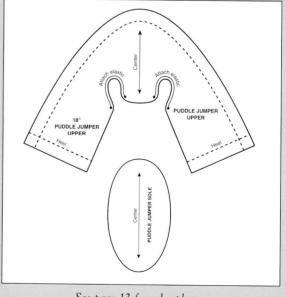

See page 13 for color photo.

Rain Hat

Sizes: To fit 18-inch, 14-inch and 8-inch dolls

Note: Instructions are given for the 18-inch size, with requirements for smaller sizes shown in brackets when applicable. When only one requirement is given, it applies to all three sizes.

Pattern Notes

Use 1/4-inch [1/8-inch for 8-inch size] seam allowance throughout unless indicated otherwise.

Set machine stitch size to 10–12 stitches per inch.

Clip all seams and curves, as indicated on pattern.

Cutting Instructions

Cut six hats and one brim from vinyl fabric.

Sewing Instructions

1. With vinyl sides together, sew three hat pieces together at side seams. Trim seams.
2. Repeat with remaining three hat pieces.
3. With vinyl sides together, sew hat sections together from one bottom edge, across the middle to other bottom edge.
4. Trim seam and finish edge with zigzag stitch.

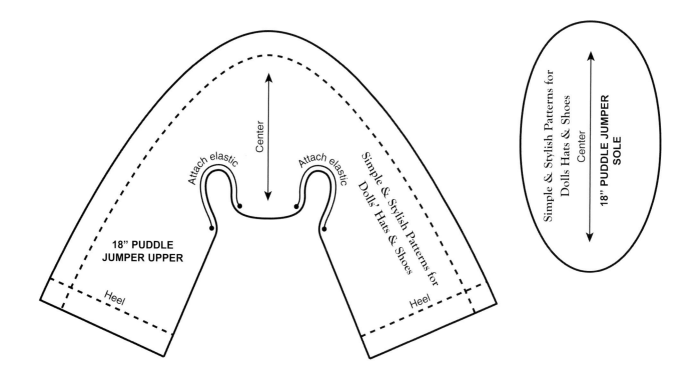

18" PUDDLE JUMPER UPPER

Attach elastic · Center · Attach elastic

Heel

Simple & Stylish Patterns for Dolls' Hats & Shoes

Heel

Simple & Stylish Patterns for Dolls' Hats & Shoes · Center · 18" PUDDLE JUMPER SOLE

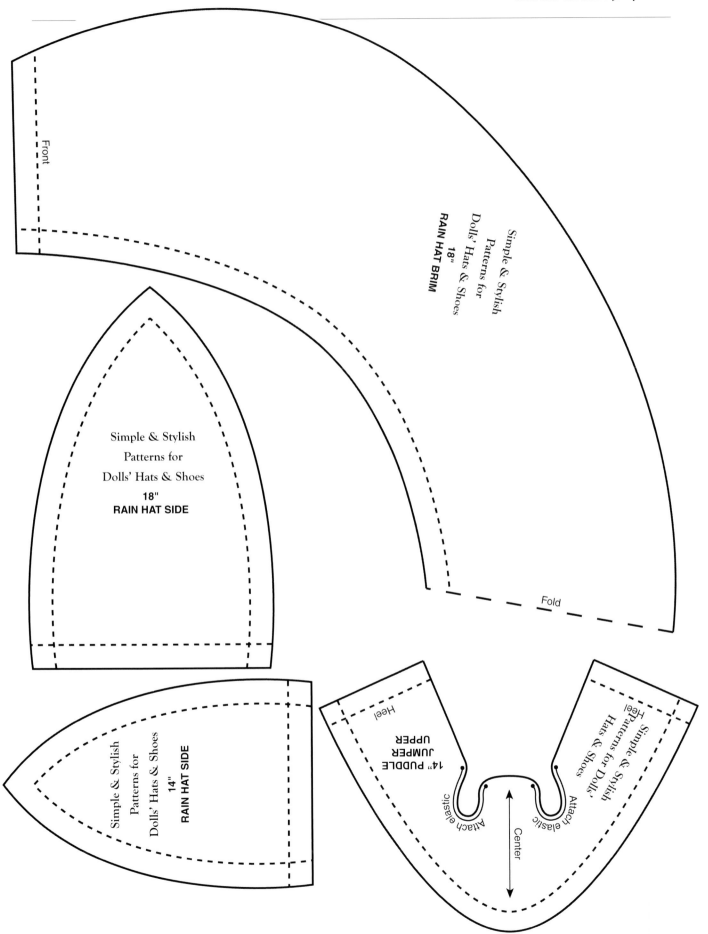

Front

Simple & Stylish
Patterns for
Dolls' Hats & Shoes
18"
RAIN HAT BRIM

Simple & Stylish
Patterns for
Dolls' Hats & Shoes
18"
RAIN HAT SIDE

Fold

Simple & Stylish
Patterns for
Dolls' Hats & Shoes
14"
RAIN HAT SIDE

Heel

14" PUDDLE
JUMPER
UPPER

Attach elastic

Attach elastic

Center

Simple & Stylish
Patterns for Dolls'
Hats & Shoes

Heel

5. With wrong sides together, sew hat brim to hat. Trim seam and finish with zigzag stitch.

6. Sew black bias binding to edge of brim beginning and ending with front seams.

7. With right sides together and raw edges even, sew inner edge of brim to bottom edge of hat. Trim seams and finish with zigzag stitch.

8. Fold seam inside hat. Topstitch hat over seam allowance.

9. Fold brim up. Sew button on top of hat through all thicknesses to hold in place.

Puddle Jumpers

Sizes: To fit 18-inch, 14-inch and 8-inch dolls

Note: Instructions are given for the 18-inch size, with requirements for smaller sizes shown in brackets when applicable. When only one requirement is given, it applies to all three sizes.

Instructions

1. Cut two uppers and two soles. Glue soles to lightweight cardboard. Let dry. Trim excess cardboard.

2. Place elastic on wrong side of openings on uppers. Sew in place using zigzag stitch around opening edges.

3. Sew 1/4 inch [1/8 inch for 8-inch size] from bottom edge of upper. Zigzag heel edges to finish. With right sides together, sew heel edges together. Open seam and sew zigzag stitch across top edge to finish.

4. Apply carpet tape to cardboard sole. Peel paper backing from heel end. With cloth side of sole in shoe, matching centers, and using stitching lines as a guide, fold edge of heel over sole and press.

5. Peel paper from toe end of sole and, matching centers, fold edges over sole and press. Remove paper backing and press remaining edges in place.

6. Apply second piece of carpet tape over folded edges and trim excess. Remove paper backing and apply sole to heavy cardboard. Trim excess.

7. Cut two heels from heavy cardboard. Apply carpet tape to one side, trim away excess. Remove paper backing and adhere heel to bottom of sole.

8. Cut bias tape to fit around top edges, cutting ends at a slight angle. Apply fabric glue to inside upper edge only of shoes. Press bias tape in place over shoe top. Let dry.

9. Apply seam sealant to cut ends of bias tape.

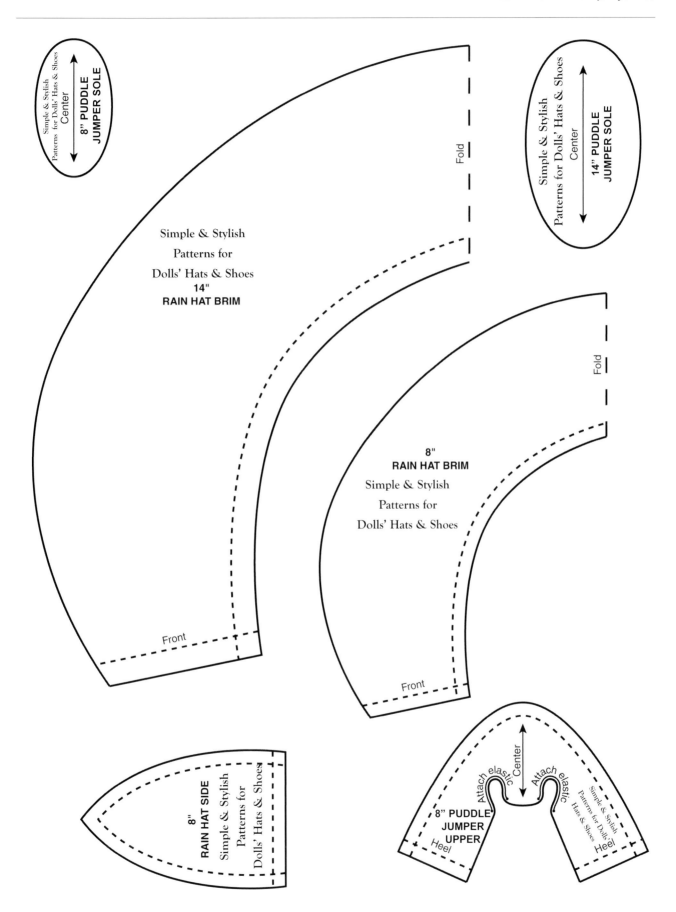

Simple & Stylish Patterns for Dolls' Hats & Shoes
Center
8" PUDDLE JUMPER SOLE

Simple & Stylish Patterns for Dolls' Hats & Shoes
Center
14" PUDDLE JUMPER SOLE

Fold

Simple & Stylish
Patterns for
Dolls' Hats & Shoes
14"
RAIN HAT BRIM

Fold

8"
RAIN HAT BRIM
Simple & Stylish
Patterns for
Dolls' Hats & Shoes

Front

Front

8"
RAIN HAT SIDE
Simple & Stylish Patterns for Dolls' Hats & Shoes

Attach elastic
Center
Attach elastic
8" PUDDLE JUMPER UPPER
Simple & Stylish Patterns for Dolls' Hats & Shoes
Heel
Heel

Sailor Hat & Canvas Slip-ons

Materials for Sailor Hat

- 1/4 yard [1/8 yard for 8-inch size] white cotton denim

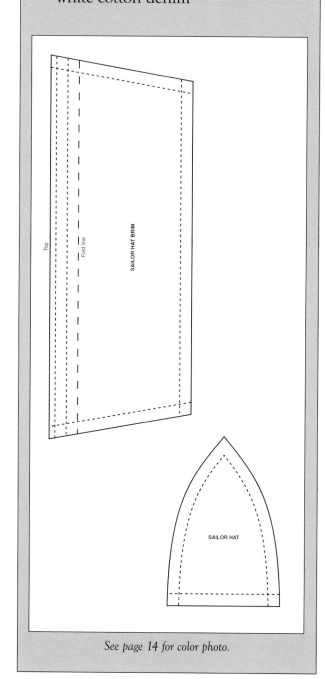

See page 14 for color photo.

Materials for Canvas Slip-ons

- 1/8 yard white cotton denim
- 1/8 yard flannel
- White craft foam (extra thick)
- Lightweight cardboard
- Fabric glue
- Blue fine-tip permanent marker
- 8 inches [6 inches for 8-inch size] 1/4-inch wide white twill tape
- 1/8 yard fusible web
- Cloth carpet tape

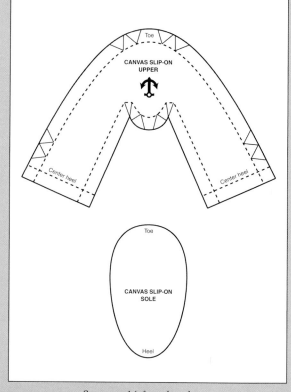

See page 14 for color photo.

Sailor Hat

Sizes: To fit 18-inch, 14-inch and 8-inch dolls

Note: Instructions are given for the 18-inch size, with requirements for smaller sizes shown in brackets when applicable. When only one requirement is given, it applies to all three sizes.

Pattern Notes

Use 1/4-inch [1/8-inch for 8-inch size] seam allowance throughout unless indicated otherwise.

Set machine stitch size to 10–12 stitches per inch.

Clip all seams and curves, as indicated on pattern.

Use zigzag or edging stitch to finish raw edges.

Cutting Instructions

Cut six hats from white cotton denim. Cut two brims from white cotton denim.

Sewing Instructions

1. With right sides together, sew three hat pieces together. Repeat with remaining three hat pieces.
2. With right sides together, sew sections together from one bottom edge, across top to other bottom edge. Trim seams. Finish raw edge with zigzag stitch. Press.
3. With right sides together, sew brims along short ends. Finish raw edges with zigzag stitch. Press seams flat.
4. Finish top raw edge of brim with zigzag stitch. Fold under 5/8 inch [3/8 inch for 8-inch size] to wrong side of brim and press.
5. Machine-stitch 1/4 inch [1/8 inch for 8-inch size] from folded edge of brim. Repeat 1/4 inch [1/8 inch for 8-inch size] from first row of stitches.
6. With right side of cuff on wrong side of hat and with bottom raw edges even, sew brim to hat. Finish raw edge with zigzag stitch.
7. Turn brim out; press seam down. Fold brim up about 1½ inches [3/4 inch for 8-inch size]. Press folded edge.

Canvas Slip-ons

Sizes: To fit 18-inch, 14-inch and 8-inch dolls

Note: Instructions are given for the 18-inch size, with requirements for smaller sizes shown in brackets when applicable. When only one requirement is given, it applies to all three sizes.

Instructions

1. Cut two uppers from white cotton denim. Cut two uppers from flannel.

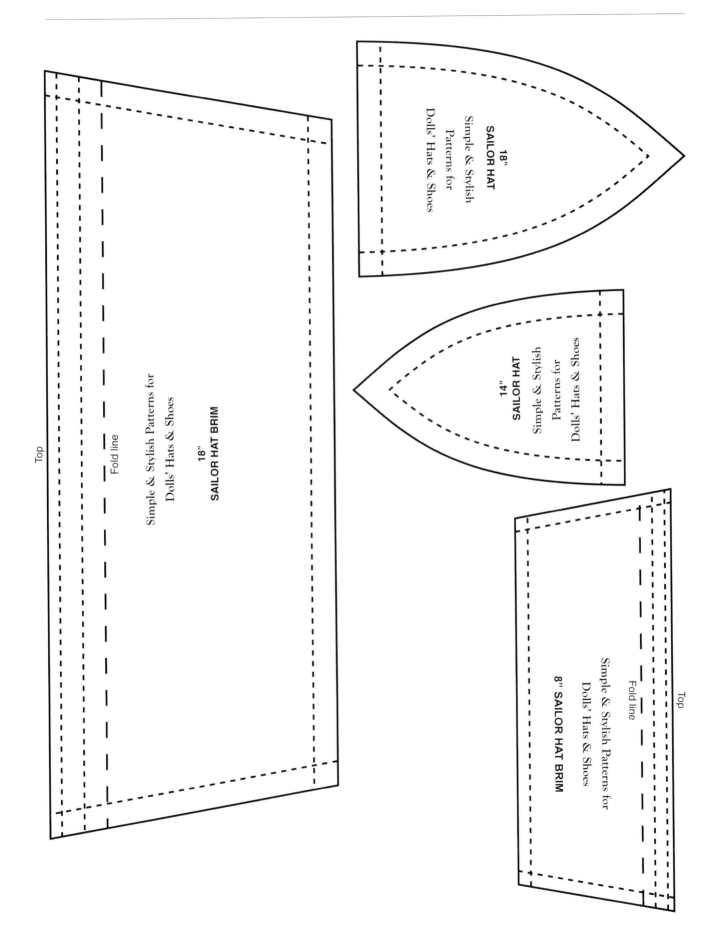

Top

Fold line

Simple & Stylish Patterns for
Dolls' Hats & Shoes

**18"
SAILOR HAT BRIM**

**18"
SAILOR HAT**
Simple & Stylish
Patterns for
Dolls' Hats & Shoes

**14"
SAILOR HAT**
Simple & Stylish
Patterns for
Dolls' Hats & Shoes

Simple & Stylish Patterns for
Dolls' Hats & Shoes

8" SAILOR HAT BRIM

Fold line

Top

Using transfer paper, trace anchor pattern on denim uppers as indicated on pattern. Outline and fill in with fine-point blue permanent marker.

2. Trace two soles on paper side of fusible web. Cut out just outside traced lines and remove paper backing. Following manufacturer's instructions, fuse to white flannel and cut out on traced lines.

3. Fuse bonded flannel with lightweight cardboard. Cut out. Apply carpet tape to cardboard side of soles. Trim excess. Set aside.

4. Sew flannel uppers to denim uppers around upper edge. Clip corners at curved instep. Trim seam allowance around curve to reduce bulk. Turn right side out and press. Topstitch close to seam.

5. Finish raw edges of heels with zigzag stitch. Stitch around bottom of uppers 1/4 inch [1/8 inch for 8-inch size] from edge. Trim flannel uppers close to seam. Clip curves around heel and toe. Peel tape backing from heel end of sole.

6. With fabric side of sole on inside of upper, using stitching lines as guides and, matching centers, fold heel edge of upper over sole and adhere to tape.

7. Peel tape backing from toe end of sole. Fold toe edge of upper over sole and adhere to tape. Remove remaining tape backing and press edges of upper to sole around entire sole.

8. Adhere second piece of carpet tape to bottom of sole covering folded edges. Trim excess. Remove tape backing and adhere to extra-thick craft foam. Trim close to sole edge.

9. Apply fabric glue to edge of foam sole. Wrap 1/4-inch wide white twill tape around sole, overlapping ends at back. Allow glue to dry.

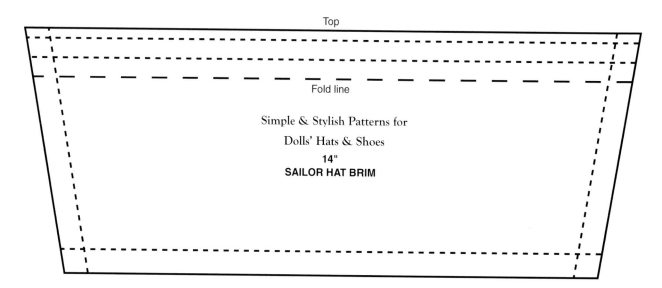

Top

Fold line

Simple & Stylish Patterns for

Dolls' Hats & Shoes

14"

SAILOR HAT BRIM

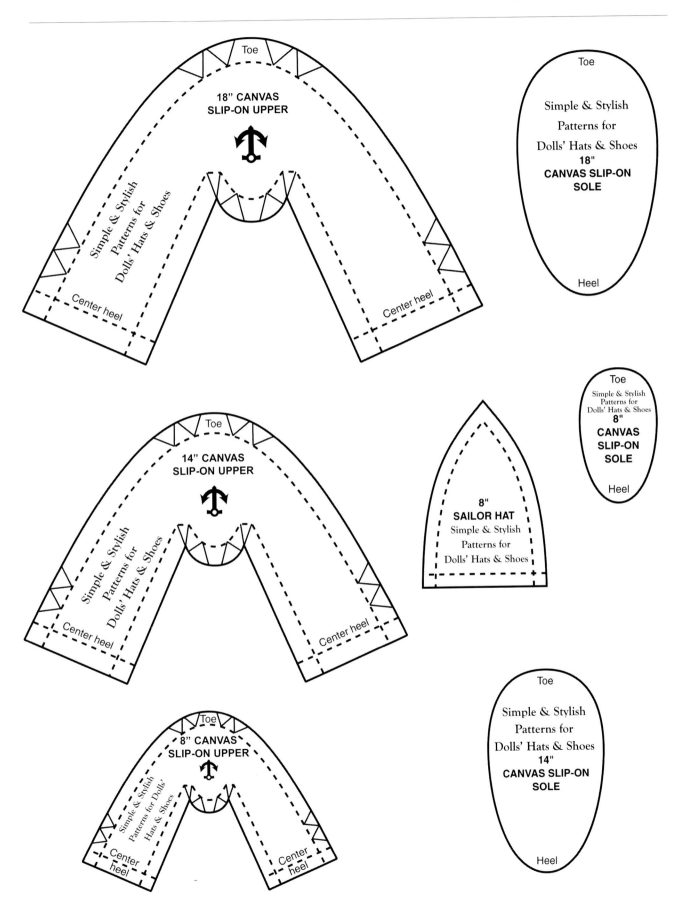

Toe

18" CANVAS SLIP-ON UPPER

Simple & Stylish
Patterns for
Dolls' Hats & Shoes

Center heel

Center heel

Toe

Simple & Stylish
Patterns for
Dolls' Hats & Shoes
**18"
CANVAS SLIP-ON
SOLE**

Heel

Toe

14" CANVAS SLIP-ON UPPER

Simple & Stylish
Patterns for
Dolls' Hats & Shoes

Center heel

Center heel

Toe

Simple & Stylish
Patterns for
Dolls' Hats & Shoes
**8"
CANVAS
SLIP-ON
SOLE**

Heel

**8"
SAILOR HAT**
Simple & Stylish
Patterns for
Dolls' Hats & Shoes

Toe

8" CANVAS SLIP-ON UPPER

Simple & Stylish
Patterns for Dolls'
Hats & Shoes

Center heel

Center heel

Toe

Simple & Stylish
Patterns for
Dolls' Hats & Shoes
**14"
CANVAS SLIP-ON
SOLE**

Heel

Summer Hat & Sandals

Materials for Summer Hat

- 1/4 yard [1/8 yard for 8-inch size] fabric
- 1/4 yard [1/8 yard for 8-inch size] medium-weight interfacing
- 1/4 yard [1/8 yard for 8-inch size] fusible web
- Dimensional fabric paint (optional)

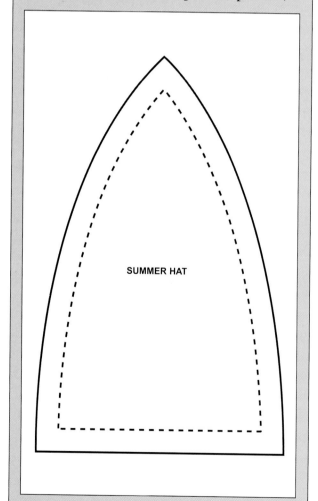

See page 5 for color photo.

Materials for Sandals

- 1/4 yard [1/8 yard for 8-inch size] summer hat fabric
- 1/4 yard [1/8 yard for 8-inch size] fusible web
- Lightweight cardboard
- Fabric glue
- Craft foam
- Cloth carpet tape
- Dimensional fabric paint (optional)
- Spring clothespins (optional)

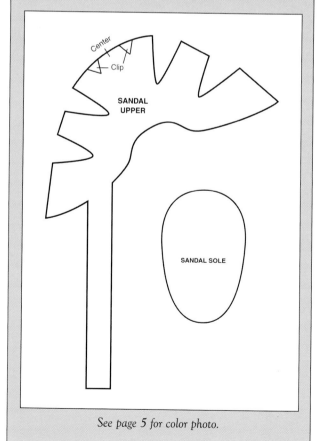

See page 5 for color photo.

Summer Hat

Sizes: To fit 18-inch, 14-inch and 8-inch dolls

Note: Instructions are given for the 18-inch size, with requirements for smaller sizes shown in brackets when applicable. When only one requirement is given, it applies to all three sizes.

Pattern Notes

Use 1/4-inch [1/8-inch for 8-inch size] seam allowance throughout unless indicated otherwise.

Set machine stitch size to 10–12 stitches per inch.

Clip all seams and curves, as indicated on pattern.

Use zigzag or edging stitch to finish raw edges.

Cutting Instructions

Trace six hat sides on paper side of fusible web. Cut out just outside traced lines. Following manufacturer's instructions, fuse to fabric. Cut out on traced lines. Remove paper backing to medium-weight interfacing.

Sewing Instructions

1. With right sides together, sew three hat sides together. Finish seam edges with zigzag stitch. Press. Repeat with remaining three hat sides.

2. With right sides together, sew both hat side sections together in one continuous seam to form hat top. Finish seam edges with zigzag stitch. Press.

3. For ruffle, cut 25-inch x 3-inch [13½-inch x 1-1/2-inch for 8-inch size] strip from fabric. With right sides together, sew short ends to form circle. With wrong sides together, sew gathering stitch 1/4 inch from raw edge.

4. Pull gathering stitches to fit bottom of hat top. Adjust gathers. Sew ruffle to hat with raw edges even. Trim seam slightly.

5. Finish edges with zigzag stitch. Pull ruffle down and fold seam allowance to inside. Sew through seam allowance close to stitching.

6. With dimensional fabric paint, randomly apply dots and squiggles on hat, let dry.

Sandals

Sizes: To fit 18-inch, 14-inch and 8-inch dolls

Note: Instructions are given for the 18-inch size, with requirements for smaller sizes shown in brackets when applicable. When only one requirement is given, it applies to all three sizes.

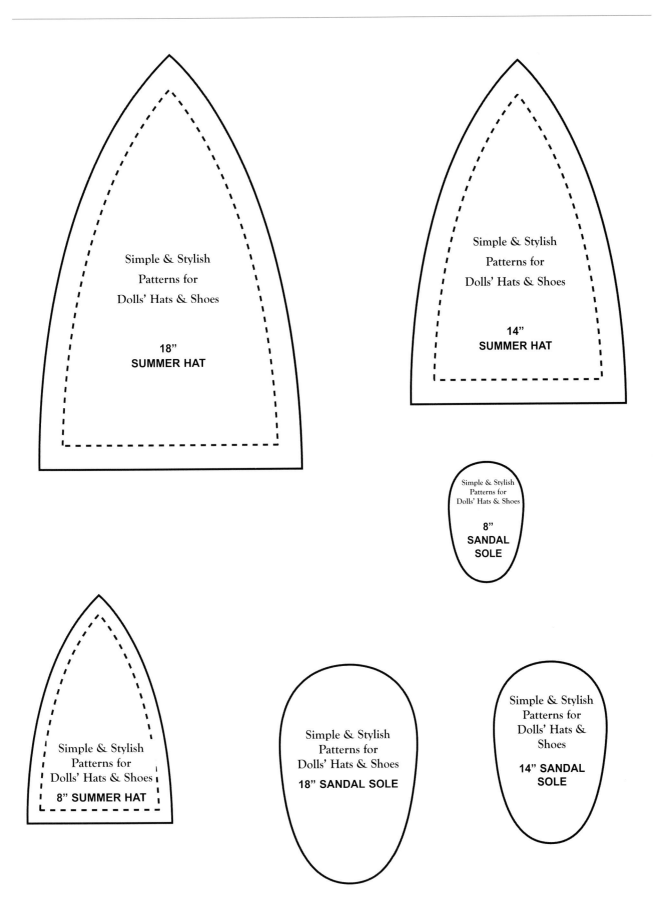

Simple & Stylish
Patterns for
Dolls' Hats & Shoes

18"
SUMMER HAT

Simple & Stylish
Patterns for
Dolls' Hats & Shoes

14"
SUMMER HAT

Simple & Stylish
Patterns for
Dolls' Hats & Shoes

8"
SANDAL
SOLE

Simple & Stylish
Patterns for
Dolls' Hats & Shoes
8" SUMMER HAT

Simple & Stylish
Patterns for
Dolls' Hats & Shoes
18" SANDAL SOLE

Simple & Stylish
Patterns for
Dolls' Hats &
Shoes

14" SANDAL
SOLE

Instructions

1. Trace two sandal uppers and two sandal soles on paper side of fusible web. Cut out just outside traced lines. Remove paper backing. Following manufacturer's instructions, fuse to wrong sides of fabric. Cut out on traced lines. Remove paper backing.

2. Fuse uppers to wrong sides of fabric. Fuse soles to lightweight cardboard. Cut out. Clip toes as indicated on pattern.

3. Adhere cloth carpet tape to cardboard side of sole. Trim excess.

4. For first shoe, peel tape backing from heel end of sole. With fabric side of sole in upper, matching centers, fold approximately 1/4 inch [1/8 inch for 8-inch size] of heel edge of upper over sole and adhere to tape.

5. Peel tape backing from toe end of sole. Fold toe edge of upper over sole in same manner and adhere to tape. Remove remaining tape backing and press edges of upper to sole around entire shoe.

6. Repeat steps 4 and 5 for second shoe, reversing upper.

7. Adhere another piece of carpet tape to sole bottoms, covering folded edges. Remove tape backing and adhere craft foam. Trim close to edges.

8. If desired, apply dimensional fabric paint around sole edges. Outline edges of sandals. Let dry.

9. Adjust back strap so sandal can slip on and off doll's foot. Trim to desired length.

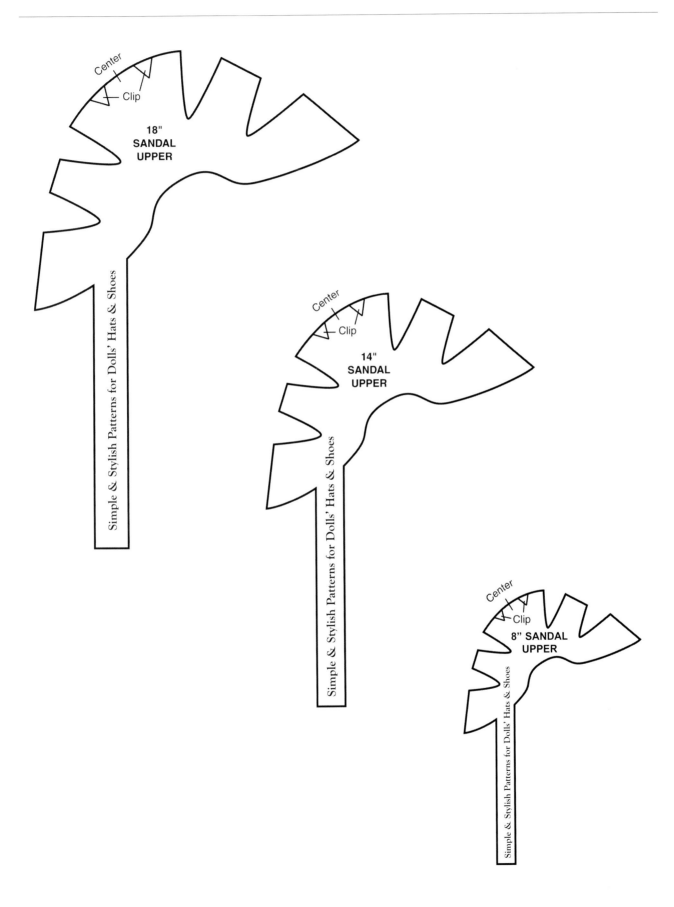

Center
Clip
18"
SANDAL
UPPER

Simple & Stylish Patterns for Dolls' Hats & Shoes

Center
Clip
14"
SANDAL
UPPER

Simple & Stylish Patterns for Dolls' Hats & Shoes

Center
Clip
8" SANDAL
UPPER

Simple & Stylish Patterns for Dolls' Hats & Shoes

Sunflower Hat & Ankle-Strap Shoes

Materials for Sunflower Hat

- 3/8 yard [1/4 yard for 8-inch size] unbleached muslin
- 25 inches [19 inches for 8-inch size] narrow cording [or piping for 8-inch size]
- Silk flower
- Hot-glue gun and glue sticks
- Sewing needle
- White thread
- Zipper foot

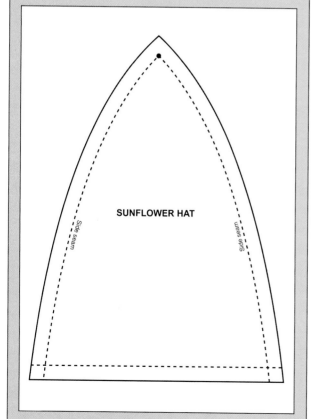

See page 15 for color photo.

Materials for Ankle-Strap Shoes

- 1/4 yard [1/8 yard for 8-inch size] unbleached muslin
- Lightweight cardboard
- 1/4 yard [1/8 yard for 8-inch size] fusible web
- Cloth carpet tape
- Needle (fine)
- White thread
- Fabric glue
- Two spring clothespins
- Craft foam
- Two snap fasteners

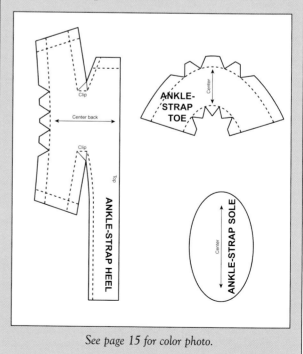

See page 15 for color photo.

Sunflower Hat

Sizes: To fit 18-inch, 14-inch and 8-inch dolls

Note: Instructions are given for the 18-inch size, with requirements for smaller sizes shown in brackets when applicable. When only one requirement is given, it applies to all three sizes.

Pattern Notes

Use 1/4-inch [1/8-inch for 8-inch size] seam allowance throughout unless indicated otherwise.

Set machine stitch size to 10–12 stitches per inch.

Clip all seams and curves, as indicated on pattern.

Use zigzag or edging stitch to finish raw edges.

Cutting Instructions

1. Cut eight hats from unbleached muslin.
2. Cut 18-inch x 1-inch [3/4-inch for 8-inch size] bias strip.

Sewing Instructions

1. With right sides together, sew four hat pieces together along side seams for hat. Press seams. Set aside.
2. With right sides together, sew four hat pieces together along side seams for lining. Press seams. Set aside.
3. Fold 18-inch x 1-inch [3/4-inch for 8-inch size] muslin strip over cording. Using zipper foot, sew edges of strip close to cording to make piping.
4. With raw edges even, sew piping to right side of hat, overlapping ends of piping at back.
5. With right sides together, sew lining to hat at bottom edge, leaving a two-inch opening for turning.
6. Turn lining inside hat. Hand-stitch opening closed.
7. Fold front of hat up as seen in illustration. Glue sunflower to front of hat.

Ankle-Strap Shoes

Sizes: To fit 18-inch, 14-inch and 8-inch dolls

Note: Instructions are given for the 18-inch size, with requirements for smaller sizes shown in brackets when applicable. When only one requirement is given, it applies to all three sizes.

Instructions

1. Trace two heels, toes and soles on paper side of fusible web and cut out just outside traced lines. Following manufacturer's instructions, fuse to unbleached muslin. Cut out on traced lines. Remove paper backing.

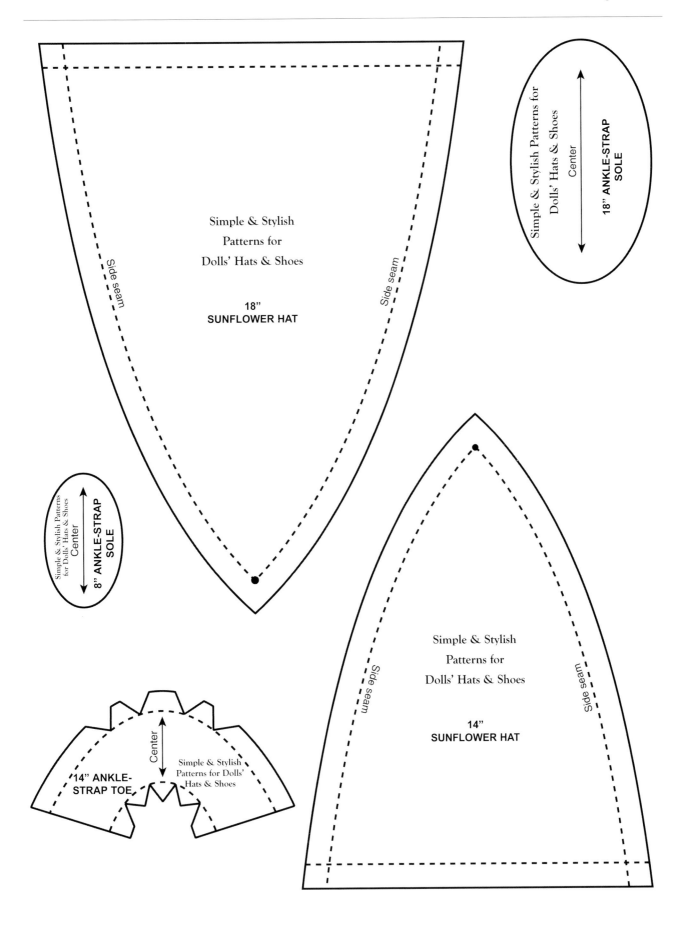

Simple & Stylish

Patterns for

Dolls' Hats & Shoes

18"
SUNFLOWER HAT

Side seam

Side seam

Simple & Stylish Patterns for
Dolls' Hats & Shoes

Center

18" ANKLE-STRAP
SOLE

Simple & Stylish Patterns
for Dolls' Hats & Shoes

Center

8" ANKLE-STRAP
SOLE

Simple & Stylish

Patterns for

Dolls' Hats & Shoes

14"
SUNFLOWER HAT

Side seam

Side seam

14" ANKLE-
STRAP TOE

Center

Simple & Stylish
Patterns for Dolls'
Hats & Shoes

2. Cut two heels and two toes from unbleached muslin. With right sides together, sew one bonded toe to one muslin toe along inner edge. Clip curve and turn right side out. Press. **Note:** *Fabric will bond.* Zigzag stitch to finish edges. Repeat with other toe.

3. With right sides together, sew one bonded heel to one muslin heel, as indicated on pattern. Clip corners. Turn right side out and press, folding extended bonded edge at top over muslin edge. **Note:** *Fabric will bond.* Sew zigzag stitch to finish raw edge including side edges.

4. With right sides together, sew one side edge of heel to side edge of toe. Press seam open and stitch across top edge of seam.

5. Stitch around bottom of shoe 1/4 inch [1/8 inch for 8-inch size] from edge. With right sides together, sew second side seam in same manner.

6. Apply carpet tape to cardboard sole. Peel paper backing from heel end. With muslin side of sole in shoe, matching centers, and using stitching lines as a guide, fold edge of heel over sole and press.

7. Peel paper from toe end of sole and, matching centers, fold edges over sole and press. Remove paper backing and press remaining edges in place.

8. Apply second piece of carpet tape over folded edges and trim excess. Remove paper backing and apply sole to heavy cardboard. Trim excess.

9. Cut two heels from craft foam. Apply carpet tape to one side, trim away excess. Remove paper backing and adhere heel to bottom of sole. Sew snap fasteners to ends of ankle straps.

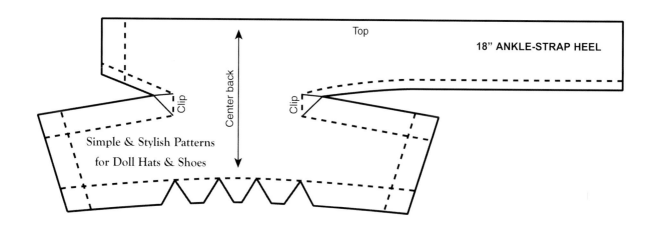

Top

18" ANKLE-STRAP HEEL

Clip

Center back

Clip

Simple & Stylish Patterns for Doll Hats & Shoes

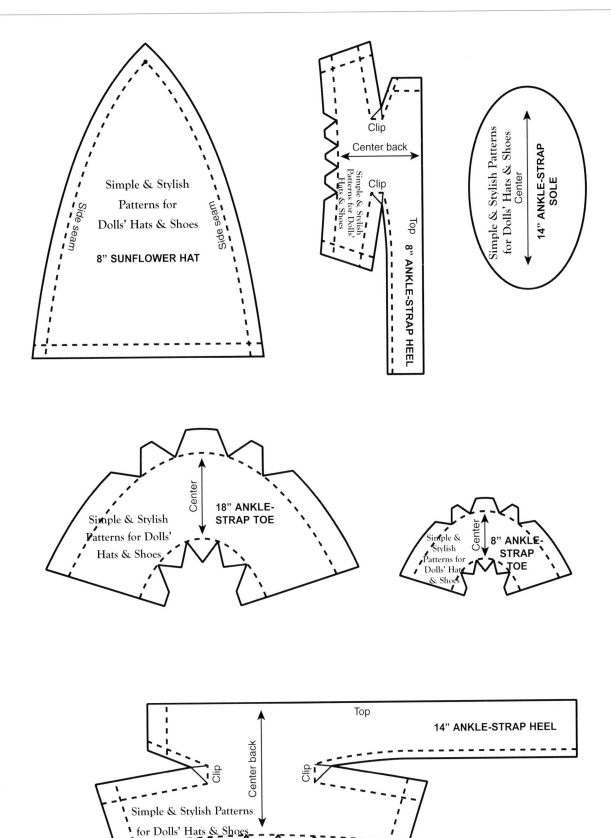

Simple & Stylish
Patterns for
Dolls' Hats & Shoes

8" SUNFLOWER HAT

Side seam

Side seam

Clip

Center back

Clip

Simple & Stylish
Patterns for Dolls'
Hats & Shoes

Top

8" ANKLE-STRAP HEEL

Simple & Stylish Patterns
for Dolls' Hats & Shoes
Center

**14" ANKLE-STRAP
SOLE**

Center

Simple & Stylish
Patterns for Dolls'
Hats & Shoes

18" ANKLE-STRAP TOE

Simple &
Stylish
Patterns for
Dolls' Hat
& Shoes

Center

8" ANKLE-STRAP TOE

Top

14" ANKLE-STRAP HEEL

Clip

Center back

Clip

Simple & Stylish Patterns
for Dolls' Hats & Shoes

Top Hat & Tap Shoes

Materials for Top Hat

- 3/8 yard [1/4 yard for 8-inch size] lightweight black fabric
- 3/8 yard [1/4 yard for 8-inch size] medium weight interfacing
- 3/8 yard [1/4 yard for 8-inch size] fusible web
- 14 inches 5/8-inch [12 inches 3/8-inch for 8-inch size] wide black satin ribbon

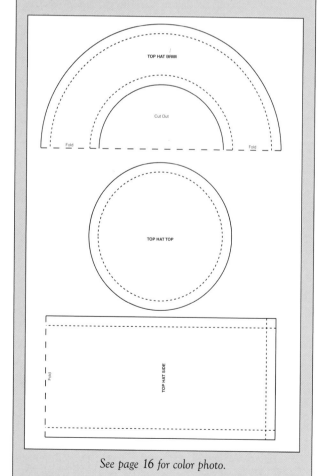

See page 16 for color photo.

Materials for Tap Shoes

- 1/4 yard [1/8 yard for 8-inch size] black satin fabric
- Lightweight cardboard
- Cloth carpet tape
- Heavy cardboard
- 1/4 yard [1/8 yard for 8-inch size] fusible web
- 24 inches 1/4-inch [20 inches 1/8-inch for 8-inch size) wide black satin ribbon

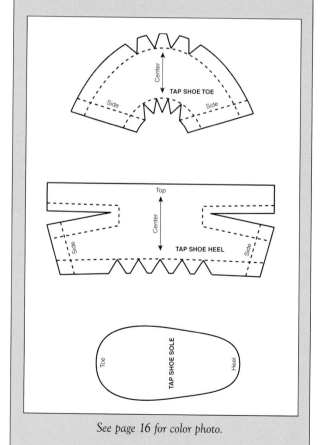

See page 16 for color photo.

Top Hat

Sizes: To fit 18-inch, 14-inch and 8-inch dolls

Note: Instructions are given for the 18-inch size, with requirements for smaller sizes shown in brackets when applicable. When only one requirement is given, it applies to all three sizes.

Pattern Notes

Use 1/4-inch [1/8-inch for 8-inch size] seam allowance throughout unless indicated otherwise.

Set machine stitch size to 10–12 stitches per inch.

Clip all seams and curves, as indicated on pattern.

Use zigzag or edging stitch to finish raw edges.

Cutting Instructions

Cut two tops, two sides and two brims from black fabric. Cut one top and one side from interfacing.

Instructions

1. Trim seam allowances from interfacing top and side.
2. Trace one brim on paper side of fusible web; cut out. Following manufacturer's instructions, fuse to interfacing. Cut out. Remove paper backing. Fuse to wrong side of one fabric brim. Sew brims, with right sides together, around outer edge. Clip curves, turn right side out and press.
3. Place three tops together with interfacing sandwiched between wrong sides of fabric. Baste.
4. With right sides together, fold each side piece, matching short edges, and sew along short edge. Trim seams and finish with zigzag stitch.
5. With wrong sides together, baste fabric sides together around one long edge. With right sides together, sew basted edge of sides to top. Trim seam; finish raw edge with zigzag stitch. Turn right side out.
6. Press seam toward top. Topstitch hat top over seam allowance. Slip interfacing side between fabric sides. Baste bottom edges of sides together.
7. With right sides together, sew inner edge of brims; trim seam and finish with zigzag stitch. Turn right side out. Press.
8. With right sides together, sew inner edge of brim to bottom edge of hat side. Trim seam and finish with zigzag stitch. Press seam inside hat. Topstitch bottom edge of hat over seam allowance.

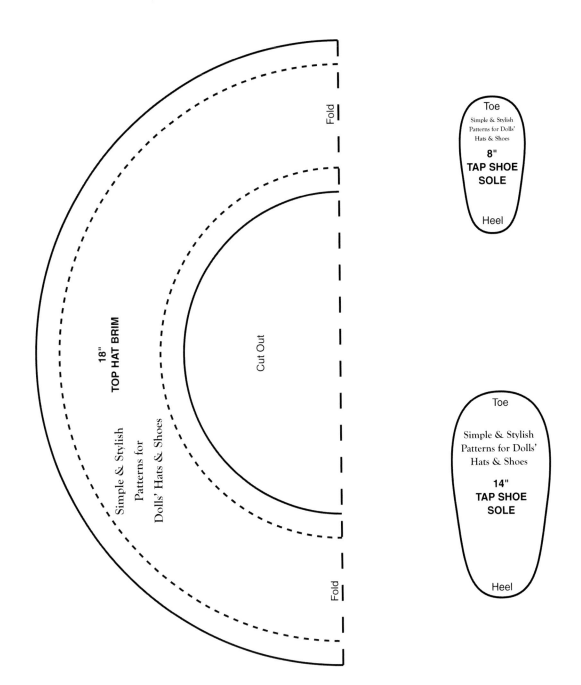

Fold

18"
TOP HAT BRIM

Simple & Stylish
Patterns for
Dolls' Hats & Shoes

Cut Out

Fold

Toe

Simple & Stylish
Patterns for Dolls'
Hats & Shoes

8"
TAP SHOE
SOLE

Heel

Toe

Simple & Stylish
Patterns for Dolls'
Hats & Shoes

14"
TAP SHOE
SOLE

Heel

9. Press brim and shape. Wrap ribbon around hat for hat band, tacking ends in place at back.

Tap Shoes

Sizes: To fit 18-inch, 14-inch and 8-inch dolls

Note: Instructions are given for the 18-inch size, with requirements for smaller sizes shown in brackets when applicable. When only one requirement is given, it applies to all three sizes.

Instructions

1. Trace two toes, two heels (reverse one), and two soles on paper side of fusible web. Cut out. Following manufacturer's instructions, fuse to wrong side of black sateen fabric; cut out. Remove paper backing. Cut two toes and two heels from black sateen fabric.

2. With right sides together, sew one bonded toe to one fabric toe on inner edge. Clip curve and turn right side out. Press. **Note:** *Fabric will bond.*

3. Machine-stitch side edges with zigzag stitch to finish. Repeat with remaining toe pieces.

4. With right sides together, sew one bonded heel to one fabric heel, as indicated on pattern. Clip corners at strap and turn right side out. Press. **Note:** *Fabric will bond.*

5. Machine-stitch side edges with zigzag stitch to finish. Trim top edge and sew zigzag stitch to finish. Repeat with remaining heel pieces.

6. With right sides together, sew toes to heels at one side. Press seam open. Stitch across top of seam. Stitch around bottom of shoe 1/4 inch [1/8 inch for 8-inch size] from edge. With right sides together, sew second side seam in same manner.

7. Apply carpet tape to cardboard sole. Peel paper backing from heel end. With flannel side of sole in shoe, matching centers and, using stitching lines as a guide, fold edge of heel over sole and press.

8. Peel paper from toe end of sole and, matching centers, fold edges over sole and press. Remove paper backing and press remaining edges in place.

9. Apply second piece of carpet tape over folded edges and trim excess. Remove paper backing and apply sole to heavy cardboard. Trim excess.

10. Cut two heels from heavy cardboard. Apply carpet tape to one side, trim away excess. Remove paper backing and

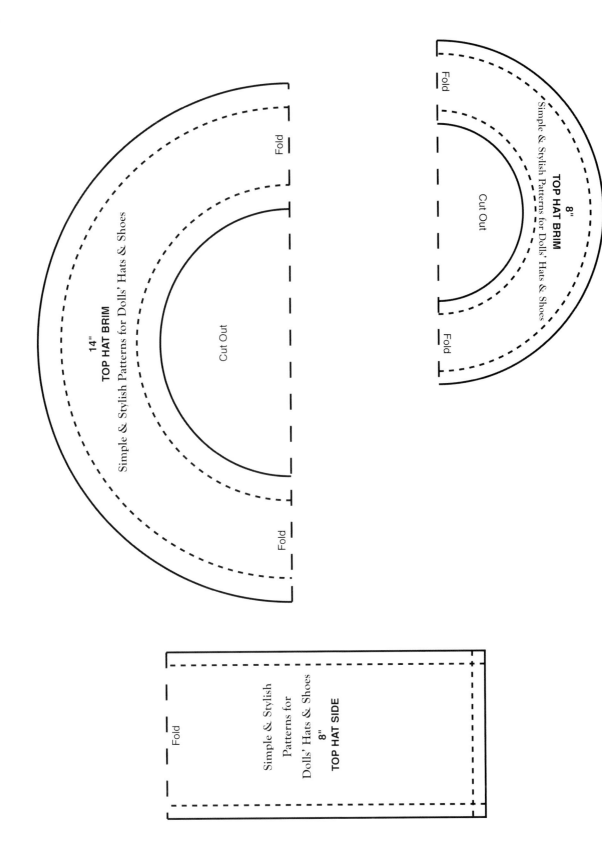

**14"
TOP HAT BRIM**
Simple & Stylish Patterns for Dolls' Hats & Shoes

Cut Out

Fold

Fold

**8"
TOP HAT BRIM**
Simple & Stylish Patterns for Dolls' Hats & Shoes

Cut Out

Fold

Fold

Simple & Stylish
Patterns for
Dolls' Hats & Shoes
**8"
TOP HAT SIDE**

Fold

adhere heel to bottom of sole.

11. Use black marker to color edges and bottoms of soles and heels.

12. Cut ribbon in fourths. Sew one end of each ribbon to end of each strap.

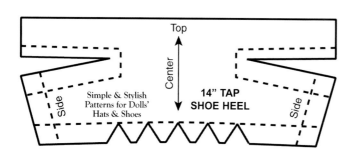

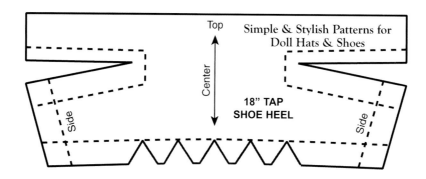

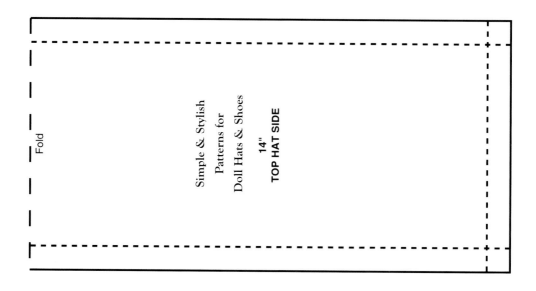

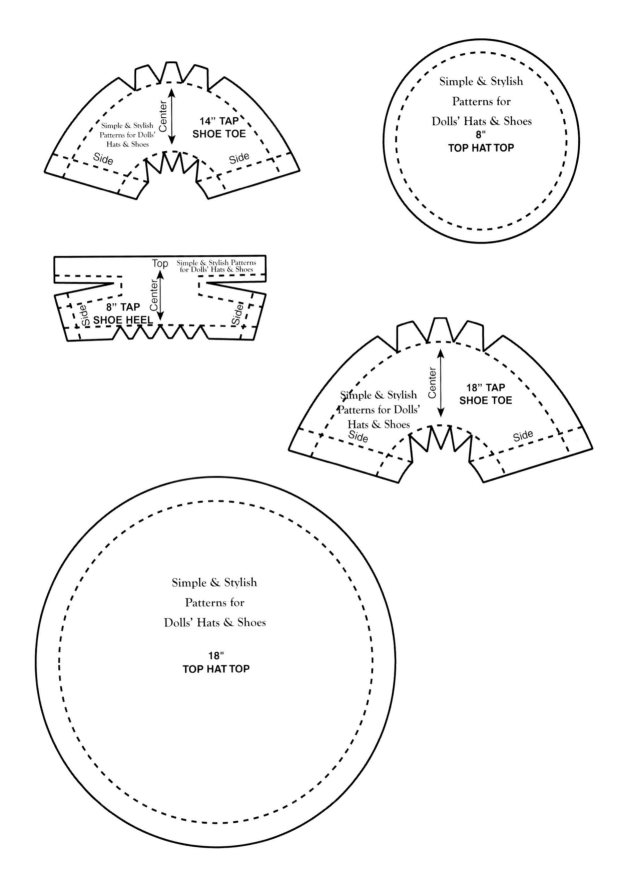

14" TAP
SHOE TOE

Simple & Stylish
Patterns for Dolls'
Hats & Shoes

Center

Side

Side

Simple & Stylish

Patterns for

Dolls' Hats & Shoes
8"
TOP HAT TOP

Top

Center

Simple & Stylish Patterns
for Dolls' Hats & Shoes

8" TAP
SHOE HEEL

Side

Side

18" TAP
SHOE TOE

Center

Simple & Stylish
Patterns for Dolls'
Hats & Shoes
Side

Side

Simple & Stylish

Patterns for

Dolls' Hats & Shoes

18"
TOP HAT TOP

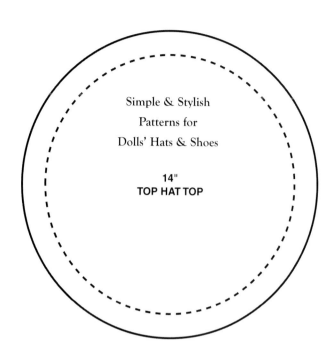

Simple & Stylish
Patterns for
Dolls' Hats & Shoes

14"
TOP HAT TOP

Center

8" TAP
SHOE TOE

Simple &
Stylish Patterns
for Doll Hats &
Shoes

Side

Side

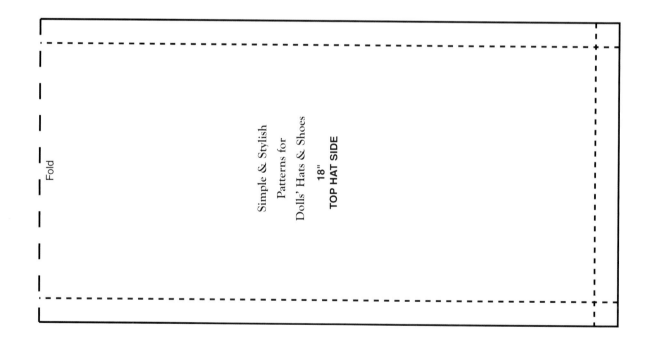

Fold

Simple & Stylish
Patterns for
Dolls' Hats & Shoes
18"
TOP HAT SIDE

Portfolio Press Creative Crafters Series

Simple & Stylish Patterns for 18-inch Dolls' Clothing
by Marla Freeman

Simple & Stylish Patterns for Dolls' Hats & Shoes
by Marla Freeman

A Closetful of Doll Clothes
by Rosemarie Ionker

Whimsical Teddy Bears: 15 Patterns & Design Techniques
by Neysa A. Phillippi

Also available from Portfolio Press

Porcelain Doll Design and Creation
by Brigitte Von Messner

Restoring Teddy Bears and Stuffed Animals
by Christel and Rolf Pistorius